Raise the Roof...

With Praise & Prayer

Mary Barrett

iUniverse, Inc.
New York   Bloomington

iUniverse books may be ordered through booksellers or by contacting:

*iUniverse
1663 Liberty Drive
Bloomington, IN 47403
www.iuniverse.com
1-800-Authors (1-800-288-4677)*

*Because of the dynamic nature of the Internet, any Web addresses or
links contained in this book may have changed since publication and
may no longer be valid. The views expressed in this work are solely those
of the author and do not necessarily reflect the views of the publisher,
and the publisher hereby disclaims any responsibility for them.*

*ISBN: 978-1-4401-7783-5 (sc)
ISBN: 978-1-4401-7784-2 (ebook)*

Printed in the United States of America

iUniverse rev. date: 09/28/2009

Dedication

This book is dedicated to all those who trust in the Lord to meet their needs and continually keep words of praise on their lips. May we always offer a grateful heart of thanksgiving to our gracious Lord and Provider.

Table of Contents

Invitation

2 Chronicles 7:14-16 (NLT*) – " Then if my people who are called by my name will humble themselves and pray and seek my face and turn from their wicked ways, I will hear from heaven and will forgive their sins and heal their land. I will listen to every prayer made in this place, for I have chosen this Temple and set it apart to be my home forever. My eyes and my heart will always be here."

Together we are about to embark on a wonderful journey into the experience of relationship, worship, and communication with God. In this study we will work to develop a face-to-face transparent union with the Holy Spirit. As we develop and practice a lifestyle of intentional spiritual communication, the desire to live a Christ-centered life begins to flourish. Together we will gain an understanding that praise is the practice we must employ to express our love and awe of God, while prayer is the vessel we use to receive the blessings, gifts, and graces from God. A life dedicated to active praise and prayer will proclaim to others the message that Jesus Christ alone provided the way for our salvation and; therefore, He alone is worthy of our deepest adoration and devotion.

"…for I have chosen this Temple and set it apart to be my home forever." Consider the invitation issued in those few words. The Bible says that each of us is God's living Temple (1 Corinthians 6:19-20) and that our lives and bodies should be poured out as a sacrifice to Him because of the sacrifice of blood that flowed from the body of Jesus for us. His people are chosen apart from all others as the place in which the spirit of God will make His home forever. Once we establish His residence in us, we have the eyes and heart of God upon us and within us forever. Have you ever considered what essential practices we must assume to maintain ourselves as holy places where God's glory can dwell? We learn that God desires those called by His name to humble themselves by praying, seeking His face in worship, and turning from wicked ways in deliverance. As we do so, God will be delighted in the songs of joy that are alive in our hearts and listen to the cries of pain that plague us as we call out to be saved. Hear it again… "I will listen to every prayer made in this place…."

We read in the Bible that the body will become a Temple and a home of God. Now picture a place you call home. Does this create a feeling of comfort, rest, familiarity, safety, and acceptance? Now imagine that we are at home with God and God chooses to be at home with us! Jesus stood in the Temple courts defending His actions once again to the religious leaders. He had just finished clearing the Holy Temple, which was His Father's house, from every kind of wickedness, corruption, and filthiness. He announced with authority that this earthy Temple will be destroyed but that He would raise it up in three days. (John 2:19-24) The newly built Temple to which He was referring was in fact His body, after His death upon the cross. Jesus' death has brought God into each one of us. Old foundations were removed and a new foundation was constructed. Temples here on earth, built by man, will not stand forever but will be brought down. Once we, as Christians, are raised again in new life; God will make our bodies the home in which He resides. Our bodies are to be maintained in holiness, purity, and oneness by opening every room to God, so that, the Spirit of Christ can enter in. We need to generate an attitude of passion for God's house within us as we welcome Him in our lives with praise and petition. He tells us that once we know each other and are joined together, He will listen to every prayer made in this place, which is now His house! Are you excited, yet? Do you feel invited to align yourself in agreement with the Spirit? If you agree that those words deliver the invitation you been waiting to hear, then continue moving out of this temporal world and into God's eternal Temple. Devote some time to understanding why Miriam danced in the desert and why a great King such as David sought the favor and protection of the King of Kings or how a prayer from a man named Jabez, mentioned only once in the Bible, so touched the heart of God in a simple four part prayer that he was granted all that he asked. The retold stories of ancient heroes are the ones which inspire us present day saints. I have chosen new stories to tell allowing Christ's work to be evident in us today and worthy of being joined with those who were before us.

It is uncomfortable to trust someone who is a stranger or unfamiliar; it does not feel natural to be ourselves and let our guard down until they are better known to us. Many of us even feel uncomfortable in our relationship with God; we feel we just do not know Him or how to even begin. The action of praise and prayer brings us into intimate fellowship with the spiritual world and the existence of God. Can you picture being so closely involved with heaven that you can begin to live it here on earth? It is not for the benefit of God that we get to know Him; after all He created man so that every man would choose to know Him. "And the very hairs on your head are all numbered" (Matthew 10:30).

Building that foundation of trust and belief is what the practice of spending daily time with God's word offers to us. As we immerse our hearts in His presence, a new and different nature emerges in us. We cannot be separate from our heavenly Father if we want a life that is pleasing to God. The role model of the life of Jesus was one in which each earthly breath was taken in unison with God. Praise and prayer were the only two things on His lips, even when facing the agony of His cruel death. Jesus was steadfast in His teaching that He and the Father were one, despite hostile opposition. As He spent three years spiritually paving the road for His disciples to follow, He pointed always to the One who sent Him. His conviction came through in His own words: "But I do nothing without consulting the Father..." (John 5:30) In these words we identify a new challenge; do we take everything to God in prayer before we take action based on our own understanding? How different would our situations be if we took the time to engage in a conversation with God and seek counsel first and act second? This drastic difference is why we are given the invitation to place prayer on the top of our priority list and praise in the front of our mind.

Is it the face of God you are seeking? Are you longing to see Him, hear Him, and know that He is right there beside you? Let's now accept the invitation and begin to place Christ at the center of our hearts as we talk to and hear from the Lord. Make these words your first prayer as you bring your offering of worship before the Holy One of heaven!

Psalm 27:4 & 8

"One thing have I desired -the thing I desire the most is to live in the house of the Lord all the days of my life, delighting in the Lord's perfections and meditating in His Temple." My heart has heard you say, "Come and talk with me." And my heart responds, "Lord, I am coming."

- The Biblical references made throughout this book are taken from the New Living Translation (NLT) version, unless specified otherwise.

Introduction

There are several things that we want to keep in our minds as we begin to better understand the benefits and blessings of using the methods of praise and prayer in our lives to connect with God at the deepest level. First, we must understand that prayer is power and praise is assurance that God is right where we need Him to be – on His throne. Second, the life of a Christian saint is motivated by awareness to sustain an unbreakable connection with God. That level of constant involvement with a spiritual walk is also known as a prayer life. A life of active prayer is lived out by consulting God first in all you do. Third, keeping the temple of the living God, our bodies, pure is the only way that the Holy Spirit will come and make a difference in us. Fourth, we must desire the presence of the Lord. The way to do that is to maintain a life of daily prayer and a heart filled with praise.

The fruit our lives bear is of great importance to the abundance of fulfillment we will feel. Book One of the Mother in Love series, *Hanging on the Vine*, explained each characteristic a healthy spiritual life needs and why. We cannot have a productive life without planting and growing positive habits. Why does it seem that, after doing everything we know how to do, things still do not seem right in our world? That is where book two just took us, *Back to the Beginning*. In it we are reminded of what we love about having a relationship with Jesus. This study looked at how far we stray when we get distracted and forget the good things that God has already given us. We get knocked off course and need to find Him again.

Now it is time to elevate ourselves and one another to the next level on this path of spiritual development on which we have embarked. Once we have repented and turned back to communion with God, how do we remain there? He has been gracious and delivered us back to friendship, allowing us to assume the responsibility to live with a new nature, as the old is gone. Receiving a new nature means we pursue God's way of life. We cannot function in the spiritual world unless we have a prayerful life that circulates God's spirit through us and back out to others. Prayers that make a difference go upward to heaven and are lived outward here to impact the world. Conversation with God is our link to a Christ-centered life.

If I could share only one verse to illustrate the theme of the message contained in this study, it would be 1 Chronicles 28:8-10. "....get to know the God of your ancestors. Worship and serve Him with your whole heart and with a willing mind. For the Lord sees every heart and understands and knows every plan and thought." My prayer is that we will learn together and that through praising God with a grateful heart and praying to God with pure and open minds will we be able to see amazing things and be blessed with revelation into what we have available.

Worship is that special place where praise and prayer thrive, co-existing and merging into a beautiful atmosphere of sacrifice that is pleasing and acceptable to our righteous King. A life centered on what is excellent will overflow with contentment, because we have entrusted ourselves to be totally exposed to the Source that promises to fill us up when we run dry. Introduce yourself to the Source that will empower you to be content and victorious, whatever the situation, with these words: Philippians 4: 6-7 – Don't worry about anything; instead, pray about everything. Tell God what you need and thank him for all he has done. If you do this, you will experience God's peace, which is far more wonderful than the human mind can understand. His peace will guard your hearts and minds as you live in Christ Jesus. Let's get to the Source of life by getting on our knees!

"Say Goodnight"

Like most people, I thought I had a grasp on the basics of prayer. One says grace, one thanks God for what one has, and one tells God what one needs. That should be pretty much all there is to it; it sounded good to me. However, I was once again changed by the gentle but steadfast spiritual guidance of my mother-in-law, who seized the opportunity to teach me more about some of the things that I thought I already knew. Another visual life lesson was brewing and I did not expect it. The beginning of my walk with the Lord was difficult (for both of us) because, for me, the lack of control of a situation makes me extremely anxious. So, when I found out that my husband had to go away for a while and leave me and two very young children at home, I became more than anxious. Tom and his dad had to go out of state for a week for work. We had only been married a little more than three years, and I had never been alone before, especially for that length of time. Added to the mix of "firsts" I would be experiencing, I also had responsibility over these two babies who depended on me for their survival. Things were really looking grim in my world; I panicked, and then I hatched what I believed was the perfect plan. Wasting no time, I called my mother-in-law to inform her of what I had come up with on my very own.

"Mom, the children and I are moving in for a week… isn't that going to be fun?" She let me get it all out of my system as I excitedly told her the details of what we would all do with our time together. Then she told me lovingly, "No, you can't come. You need to stay in your home."

She and I went back and forth. How could she not let us come? In my mind, this was just cruel. Didn't she love us? Didn't she understand I was scared? Both of us could be persuasive when necessary. The conversation then turned as I pleaded my case and she did not budge. I even went so far as to declare that none of us were going to make it through the week. We would not get much sleep, but that did not seem to bother her. My last stance, as a misunderstood martyr, was bravely conceding that I guess the children and I could just as easily camp out in our own living room for the week and hope for the best.

Mom was ready with a plan too, but I liked mine better. She knew I needed to use this time as a growing experience and capably run my home while my husband was gone. "Mary, here is what we are going to do. You will call me each night after the children are in bed, and we will read Psalm 91 together. You and the children are going to be fine, and everyone will sleep in their own beds. No camping. Then we will say goodnight and you will go to bed."

Well, to my amazement (and her relief) her plan worked that night and then again for the next five nights. She started each phone call by asking if the children were in bed and said that God would know if I was lying. She would then read Psalm 91 with me and I gained comfort and strength. The children and I were rested and safe, and we had a nice week. Since that period in my life, which is now over fifteen years ago, I have viewed prayer very differently. The gift I was given was the knowledge of how to use prayer as a tool in every situation. By letting my fear go and praying out loud to God, I allowed Him to bring comfort and peace to me as He revealed that we were not really alone.

Psalm 91 is a shield of protection that I could feel surrounding me each night that we read it. Those special late-night calls with my mother-in-law dwell among my most treasured memories. I encourage you to sit down and drink deep from these words into your soul and believe them. I am so grateful for all the many, many times that my mother-in-law hung in there with me in love; so that, the power of Christ was not only seen but also became forever real to me and my children. I praise the Lord that my spiritual walk has matured over the years and I don't argue quite as often. Now I have been blessed with opportunities to pray with others, offering hope and comfort by pointing to the power of Christ as the anchored rock during my tests of life.

Format of Devotions

At the conclusion of each chapter there is a section to draw you into God's Word, called Questions from the Heart. Take some time and let the Holy Spirit search your heart as you answer the questions that open the path to a prayerful life and devoted worship. This is a good exercise to do with a group or during quiet personal reflection. After you have finished exploring the questions you can move on to the section entitled Scripture to Rejoice In. More scripture is offered that pertains to the topics you have read. Go further into the message and meditate and try writing out the verses that have referenced. The blank pages after the chapter titled Personal Moments are for you to track the answers you receive and thoughts you experience.

Something that always inspires me is journaling. The moments when the Holy Spirit gives us insight are precious. Located in the back of the book you will find additional blank pages headed with A Heart of Worship. Please capture anything that has been meaningful to you there so that you can record your personal growth.

Chapter One:

Bringing More than a Song

A Piece of God's Word – "Sing to the Lord a new song. Sing His praises in the assembly of the faithful. O Israel, rejoice in your Maker. O people of Jerusalem, exalt in your King. Praise His name with dancing, accompanied by tambourine and harp." – Psalm 149:1-3

Throughout the scriptures, the magnificent nature of God is revealed. The nature of God is good and gracious to save His people. What is your personal perception of God? Is it the image of Him sitting on the throne of heaven, shouting blatant commands like a mythical idol out to strike us down with lighting bolts if we do not comply with His wishes? How different God is from our earthy Kings who demand only our forced adoration and not the love of our heart. Our heavenly King seeks to start in the heart, having what transformed on the inside lived out in jubilation on the outside. The well spring of our heart is also what motivates our devotion and what will be poured out for all to see. God does not simply want us to sing Him a song; God wants the song that we sing to

1

match the motives in which they are offered. There should be something so passionate and so alive when we worship the Creator of the universe that drives us to stand in His presence simply awestruck at the splendor. The experience can sometimes even be indescribable. The command given by the eternal King is thus: Come, now is the time to worship; for you have seen the great things I do for you!

What does all this emotional tension we possess on the inside show when it is released and lifted up to the heavens? One word will cover it – praise. This is when you hear a song of worship and it brings you to tears and you cannot understand why. But before we can experience this expression in our lives, let us see whether we cannot first understand its significance. The Bible teaches that God, through Jesus Christ, is the provider of salvation, therefore, He alone is worthy of our highest praise. Praise is the method we use in showing gratitude and thanksgiving for the wonderful kindness with which we have been ransomed. Think of the star-struck gazes we lavish on our worldly idols; people of power, prestige, and authority receive our cheers, applause, and adoration. Their fame is temporal, yet we exhaust our energy on showing them great favor. This ought to be our response when we enter into the presence of God. What should be a natural outpouring of sheer delight in our Lord is sometimes viewed as an uncomfortable ritual. But friends, praise in the assembly of the faithful is shouting without doubt that our God reigns. It is a beautiful way to express our love to God as we proclaim to the world the glory and excellence of His name. If we as spiritual ambassadors do not raise our voices in praise of Jesus as our Lord and King, the very stones and rocks will cry out. Be free to rejoice. There will be those who will rebuke an open display of uninhibited worship, but Jesus, upon His triumphal entrance into Jerusalem, as the people screamed praises to the Holy One of the Father, said, "If they keep quiet, the stones along the roads will burst into cheers." (Luke 19:40)

This idea of praise is all about the attitude we carry. I want you to think about how easy it is to sing, dance, and get excited about God when life is good. But what do we do when the world is crumbling around us? Do we still praise the Lord for His goodness and believe that He is with us in the midst of a storm? Praise carries with it unquestioned adoration in the good times and during the bad. Whether you are winning or losing, when all is stripped away, will you still choose to come and bring the Lord something that is of worth? What will our hearts choose to do?

Miriam's story

Music often moves our soul to great depths of emotion. Think how some of your favorite songs have affected you. We rejoice, reflect, rejuvenate, and radiate through the emotions of what truly moves us. That is how praise works; it motivates a heart moved by the Source of the spirit. God wants us to be moved by the goodness of His love. Maybe that is one of the keys to bringing more than a song as an offering to God. Let the music take you there, let each chord that is played on the instrument of praise strike a note of confidence that our God is the one who reigns over all. As the Spirit of Christ receives more of our attention, we can then look back over our past and realize that He has been there before we even knew it.

God has many names, but the one that would become most treasured to a young Jewish girl named Miriam is El Shaddai, or "The All-Sufficient One." Seen throughout the entire Old Testament account is the way in which God pours mighty strength into His mistreated, weak, and frail people. Miriam, at age 12, would begin to experience God as the Comforter, Satisfier, and Nourisher for her, as well as, her family. Do you remember the story about the baby in a straw basket who floated peacefully down the Nile? During this turbulent time in history, the Israelites were captives in the land of Egypt, seen only as slaves of a nation. That babe in the basket would grow to become Moses, the prophet God used to bring freedom to the people of Israel and His law to the nations.

The sufficiency God provided started on the riverbank long before it was even dreamed possible for this people to be free and one day see the Promised Land they had heard about through their ancestor's teachings. It was through Miriam that God set His plan in motion, which eventually realized the hope of freedom for the oppressed. Miriam's family suffered anguish when her mother gave birth to Moses. The king of Egypt ordered the slaughter of Jewish baby boys as a form of population control. The fate of her brother remained to be thrown into the Nile River along with all other male babies. The thought of such an action was too unbearable and Miriam's mother decided to give up her son. Her plan was to hide him in the reeds of the river bank and send him in a tar-sealed papyrus basket down the river when she believed it was safe to do so.

Miriam followed the basket down the river, and the Hebrew boy was discovered. Pharaoh's daughter was at the river bathing; unable to have children of her own, she lovingly embraced the baby. What could have been a negative situation turned into an expression of praise to God. Miriam took the chance to intervene and offered to appoint a Hebrew woman to nurse the baby. Yes, Moses was nursed by his own mother. The word *shad* is a Hebrew word that refers to a woman's breast as she nurses her child; this also implies the same kind of tender attention that God gives to people by becoming a source of nourishment for us. That is why the term El Shaddai perfectly portrays what Miriam saw. Can you imagine how her heart must have felt like exploding into song as she witnessed the gift of her mother being the one who nursed her brother? Even though the child could not grow up in his family's home, they were given the blessing of remaining a part of his life.

Songs and praise make us confident to continue when our conditions call for retreat. Moses, as a baby boy, was sentenced to death, and God was the one responsible for saving his life, but He chose to perform his will through a little girl who was not afraid to go where she needed to go and to think fast when she got there. These leadership qualities would serve her well, as God was not finished with her or her brothers! The song she brought to this experience during her youth was total trust in a God she knew had to be there. This incident clearly illustrates two of Miriam's personality qualities that continued to stay with her throughout her adult life. She had boldness and used her intelligence.

Years later, during the great Exodus out of Egypt when the Pharaoh's army and golden chariots were destroyed in the waters of the Red Sea, Miriam was there again as a witness. Miriam had developed her leadership skills and her receptiveness to be available where God placed her. Her readiness helped her become more receptive to develop the qualities that would title her a prophetess and leader of songs. Throughout the 40-year experience in the desert, she was faithful in trying to keep the spirits of the people lifted up by being filled with joy and praise for the journey they traveled, despite how difficult it was. These people needed to keep their minds focused on the assurance that God's love was enough to keep them moving toward the reward of freedom they had been promised. He gave them fire by night and led them in the clouds by day. During each trial they encountered, God was there. Only after the people saw these miracles and were spared from the waters that were brought crashing down on their enemies did the people of Israel walk safely onto dry land and understand the power of their God. It was the song Miriam sang that brought the sound of praise to the ears of God and the message to the people that the Lord reigns forever. All the women joined and offered their voices, harps, tambourine, and praised Him with dance! Miriam was the first praise and worship leader, leading the women to fully connect with their bodies, minds, and souls to bring glory to God. The heart of a nation was moved by such a simple act of offering a song and a dance on a river bank in thanksgiving for their salvation.

Then Miriam the prophet, Aaron's sister, took a tambourine, and led all the women in rhythm and dance, and Miriam sang this song:"I will sing to the Lord, for He has triumphed gloriously; He has thrown both horse and rider into the sea." (Exodus 15:20-21)

As we bring our praise to the Lord, may it be in boldness knowing that He is El Shaddai, God Almighty, and Ruler over all. The songs we sing, the music we make and the dance we perform must match the attitude in our heart. Express yourself with uninhibited thanksgiving for the magnitude of what God has given to you. Despite what it may seem, in good times and bad, your heart can be free to sing in truth and bless the name of the Lord forever. The act of bringing more than a song, just as Miriam did, allows us to pour out our love for God using all the talents and gifts bestowed on us.

Questions from the Heart

- What is your definition of praise? Does it always have to be an outward sign such as singing and dancing?

- What did Miriam do that was important in bringing honor to God?

- How do you praise God during tough times? How is the name El Shaddai relevant to you? Remember a time when God was all-sufficient for you and praise Him for it.

- Can you relate to the story of Miriam? Do you see how praising the Lord takes more than singing a sweet song? Can you understand that it takes a willing heart of deepest expression offered to the God of heaven?

- Can you list any ways that you can be creative in praising the God of the universe? We start slow, at the very core of the method of praise, so we can become involved in it and use it as another life support tool to bring us into spiritual oneness with the Center of Life.

Scripture to Rejoice In

1 Corinthians 11:2, Romans 1:16-17, Psalms 1:2, 1 John 2:27, Revelation 7:9-12

2 Corinthians 5:17, Deuteronomy 2:7, Exodus 34:29, Psalms 149:1-9, Amos 5:21-24

Heart Reflections

Heart Reflections

Chapter Two:

We Were Taught to Pray

A Piece of God's Word – "One day Jesus told his disciples a story to illustrate their need for constant prayer and to show them that they must never give up." – Luke 18:1

A prayer life is one of the main aspects of a healthy Christian walk. How can we expect to survive in this world if we are not communicating with the One who holds all the answers we are looking for? Would it not be a disastrous mistake if those on the battleground of war did not keep in constant communication with their general? Without wise direction and counsel, even a great army will run around blindly, shooting in the dark, aimlessly hoping to hit something before it hits them. God plays the role of general and protector, guarding us safely from what we cannot see. We are on the battleground of life and without spiritual guidance our chance for survival decreases. Some of us make the mistake of treating this battleground we are on as a playground and do not assume an active prayer life. We naturally want to push ahead in life based on what we know, mapping out our own plan of attack, instead of asking God to supply what we need each day. If daily communication is cut off from our top commander, we can never be sure if we are heading in the direction of victory or defeat. It often amazes me that when I feel beat up, dried up, unfulfilled and drained it is usually because I have been unfaithful in my prayer life with God. When we are in short supply of the Spirit's power, we leave ourselves vulnerable and matchless against the attacks from the enemy of this world. Any time we are about to face what potentially is viewed as painful defeat, our reaction is to give up; but, Jesus says we must look to Him for safety. Retreat will not be an option if we chose to open our entire heart and fully surrender our mind to Christ, who is the source of our victory. If we talk to Him, whatever we seek, we will find. Our lives can not have a positive direction, unless we understand God's written way - which is the Holy Bible; or, recognize His voice - which becomes familiar to us when we spend time in prayer. Without those two essential elements, cohesively applied, anything we attempt on our own will prosper for more than a temporal moment.

The act of prayer seems to cause some confusion for us until we are taught how to use it. Don't feel alone; even the elite people who walked with Jesus and were considered to be His closest friends had their own struggles and questions about prayer. My own personal understanding of the purpose of prayer is to deepen your dependence on God alone. When you seek His help to supply the very air you breathe, then you are functioning in transparent openness and your communication can flow comfortably as you reap results in your life.

I would like to discuss the point at which we learn exactly what was taught about the right way to build a life lived in the presence of the Father by the gift offered to us through prayer. The definition of prayer as stated in the NLT Bible is as follows: "Prayer is the most universally practiced yet least understood of human experiences. Prayer is one of the greatest mysteries of the Christian faith. Its simplest definition is communication with God. Yet, so often we approach prayer like a one-way telephone conversation, forgetting that God also wants to speak to us. There are all different ways to pray – on our knees or standing, silent or out loud, alone or in a group, routinely or spontaneously all day long; none making more of a difference to God than the sincerity of your heart. Prayer is the essence of a faith relationship with God; simple enough for a child, yet so profound that we spend a lifetime plumbing its depths. Prayer assumes that it is possible to have an intimate relationship with a God who hears, cares, and is equipped to act."

You may want to read that definition several times to embrace the message for us within it. By faith alone we can talk to God and accept that He is able to do more than we could ever expect to complete on our own. Psalm 33: 4-5 adds, "I prayed to the Lord, and He answered me, freeing me from all my fears. Those who look to the Lord for help will be radiant with joy; no shadows of shame will darken their faces."

Jesus – Our Teacher and Example in Prayer

I think one of our greatest concerns about prayer is the basic question: how do we pray? As already stated, Jesus' closest companions even wanted to know this. So, like a good rabbi and leader, He did indeed teach them to pray. Not only would they see how to pray, but they would also witness a prayer life that was so tightly linked to heaven that it could not ever be separated.

The Gospel account of Matthew recorded these events thus: One day as the crowds were gathering, Jesus went up the mountainside with the disciples and sat down to teach them. (Matthew 5:1) Jesus taught about many things on this particular day. The disciples had just put down their fishing nets to answer the call of Jesus to become fishers of people. (Matthew 4:18-20) Jesus knew that their decision would be powerless if He left them merely with an interesting invitation; He had to walk with them. So, He traveled throughout Galilee teaching and preaching the Good News about the Kingdom of heaven. (Matthew 4:23-25) Without that commitment to teach and be available, any decision the people made would likely remain as just an interesting idea.

Jesus began to tell the people everything they needed to know about prayer and how to talk to God. If we listen, just as that seeking crowd on that mountain did all those years ago, the secrets will be revealed to us also. Listen to the things Jesus says we must do: "When you pray, go away by yourself, shut the door behind you, and pray to your Father secretly." (Matthew 6:6) I believe Jesus taught this so that we would be careful to be genuine with God when we are alone. There is no need to go on and on with our words, because we cannot impress God. This leads to a crucial fault that we can sometimes be guilty of – babbling. "They think their prayers are answered only by repeating their words again and again. Don't be like them, because your heavenly Father knows exactly what you need even before you ask Him!" (Matthew 6:7-8) Jesus tells us that we must pray intentionally speaking to God what is in our hearts instead of what is on our lips.

The whole lesson on how to pray was summed up as Jesus laid out the exact formula that is guaranteed success when we pray. His precise words are, "Pray like this…" (Matthew 6:9). These words are what we know as the Lord's Prayer or the Our Father. Does it surprise you that something a lot of us say methodically all the time is actually the very way Jesus says we are to approach a conversation with God in prayer? The many versions of the Bible that we have available to read present these words in different ways, but they all convey only one meaning found in the same text of Matthew 6:9-13. Meditate on that passage and practice the instructions of that model prayer. Acknowledge God with honor, thank Him for what He provides, and use His strength in your weakness. Jesus wants it to be clear to us that it is not our religion or the correct words that get our prayers heard, but the love of God. Utilize the wisdom in these words as everything Jesus taught that a perfect prayer ought to be. "Our Father who art in heaven, Hallowed be your name. Thy Kingdom come, Thy will be done on earth as it is in Heaven. Give us this day our daily bread and forgive us our debts, just as we forgive our debtors. And lead us not into temptation, but deliver us from the evil one." (NIV Bible Version)

There are still aspects of prayer that we learn as we grow spiritually and through understanding how to talk to God, we can start living an interactive prayer life and nurture it. The best teaching method in my opinion still remains by example and modeling what we hope others will follow. Jesus gave us an example of his words when He prayed alone on the Mount of Olives. Reading the Apostle Luke's account, as stated in Chapter 22 verses 39-46, we find a passionate demonstration of prayer. This happened only a very short time before Jesus was betrayed, found guilty and punished for charges of which He was innocent. Jesus had just shared in the Passover supper with His disciples representing what would happen to His body. As Jesus left from where He was, he accepted all that was ahead for Him to endure. (Luke 22:7-30)

The heart-wrenching sorrow Jesus felt was purged to God in prayer. Jesus looked for help from His heavenly Father in His darkest hour. With His faithful crew of men just a stone's throw away, Jesus, the Son of God, bent His knees in unashamed need. "Father, if you are willing, take this cup of suffering away from me. Yet I want your will, not mine" (Luke 22:42). Prayer is the act of asking God to get us through what we are facing and even take it away if it is possible; but, the result of prayer is obtaining the desire to accept what God wants and believing that He is in control. Please do not misinterpret prayer as an easy solution or a quick fix to a problem; remember that it is the most personal way we infuse God's power in every situation.

Another aspect of prayer we notice in the garden where Jesus knelt is the depth that His soul was involved with what He was asking. This prayer went beyond the words spoken, as Jesus anguished to convey His heart. Scripture tells us that He prayed more fervently and he was in such agony of spirit that his sweat fell to the ground like drops of blood. (Luke 22:44) Can there really have been such a prayer? Most of us will not experience such a prayer; but, we can certainly pray with intensity. Intensity in prayer is in our ability to continue and not stop until we are sure that we have heard from God. Jesus asked three times for the cup of suffering to be taken away and only when He was sure that it was the Father's will to continue in His mission did He end His pleading. Nothing would distract the communion between heaven and earth until His prayer was done. At last he stood up and returned to His disciples. (Luke 22:45) The will of God was brought upon Him even as He approached the mob; led by His betrayer, Judas. So, as we study this example, we see that the outcome was not that anything was prevented, but that Jesus had the confidence to face what was about to happen because the will of God was assured. If we accept what God wants for our lives, then we have truly understood prayer. May your prayer be like that of the prayer in Gethsemane; in a quiet place as you face God, spill your pain, and be prepared to listen. In chapter ten we will re-open the last night of Jesus and dig deeper into the meaning of His prayer.

Questions from the Heart

- Do you believe there is a right and wrong way to pray?

- Can you think of a time that you were intimidated by the act of prayer? Do you still feel that way? If not, what helped you grow in your prayer life?

- Is prayer a high priority in your life? Do you think that we need to pray every day as Christians? Are there special things you do that make you feel closer to God's presence? Do you communicate in a heart-to-heart relationship with God as you pray?

- What are the things Jesus says that we should pray for? Read Matthew 6:9-13 again. What makes this a model prayer?

- List what you learned from what Jesus taught and modeled about prayer through this chapter based on the references found in the Gospels of Matthew and Luke.

Scripture to Rejoice in

John 14:1, Proverbs 20:25, Exodus 20:7, Philippians 1:20-42, Psalms 22:24 & 103:13

2 Corinthians 1:4, Hebrews 4:15, Ezra 7:6-10, 1 Corinthians 15:57, Colossians 4:2

Heart Reflections

Heart Reflections

Chapter Three:

Having a Heart for Worship

A Piece of God's Word – "But the time is coming and is already here when true worshipers will worship the Father in spirit and in truth. The Father is looking for anyone who will worship him that way. For God is Spirit, so those who worship him must worship in spirit and in truth." – John 4: 23-24

Only very recently did I begin to understand fully the idea that worship is not just about clapping your hands and singing religious songs. What does it mean to worship God in spirit and in truth? We sometimes get caught up in the ceremony of worship; we do not always look to its full meaning. The center of all worship, whether communally or privately, is a genuine outpouring of reverence and gratitude for the salvation given through Jesus. As Jesus taught the Samaritan woman at the well, the time comes when it does not matter where you go to worship (John 4:19-22) and worship becomes all about the heart that is brought to God in open and humble adoration. What should be completely evident to a believer is that worship does not take place where we are; but, who we are by the grace of a loving God. Let's ask ourselves honestly, "Do I have a heart of worship?" If a human's heart is missing, the rest of the body cannot function. The heart pumps blood to the rest of the body, keeping it alive. Just as worship is the lifeline that keeps our spiritual life inflated with the Source that provides eternal life.

We need to be able to appreciate the message before it can impute any valuable meaning. If we cannot comprehend an idea, we are not likely to try to apply or use it for ourselves. As we expand our time learning in God's Word, the Bible teaches us the basics of what worship is, what it is for and how we can experience it. Worship is a behavior displayed to ascribe an ultimate value to an object, person, or being. People will order the priorities of their lives around what they worship. Think of the young people who scream and cast themselves in devotion at the stage of their favorite rock-star idol; or, those who sit at the foot of a ceramic creation in their living room, quietly surrounded in the glow of a candlelit shrine. We all participate in one form of worship or another. Human beings were created to worship. Here is what clearly defines the act of worshiping in spirit and truth. Without exception the Bible teaches that God alone is worthy of our worship. Based on that statement, we are blowing hot air into the wind if our worship is spent on something other than the glory and pleasure of God. No matter how great the pressure or temptation we must never devote our worship to other gods. To experience authentic worship, kneeling in humble adoration and rejoicing in celebration become necessary as we respond to the spiritual leading of our awakened heart. The holiness of God comes alive as we respectfully fall down before Him and worship. Psalm 95:1-7 (paraphrased) tells us to come and sing to the Lord. Let us give a joyous shout to the rock of our salvation. For the Lord is a great God, the great King above all gods. Come let us worship and bow down. Let us kneel before the Lord our maker. Follow that blueprint and your devotion will not be restrained or superficial. I promise you that if you reach upward towards heaven, using the foundation of Scripture, the fire of the Holy Spirit will reach down to you and into your soul.

A Keystone Ministry

When the passion of worship has left, you will know it. You may not realize it right away, but eventually you will feel the emptiness that wants to be filled. People want to be moved to action, inspired to continue, encouraged to be bold, and brought from brokenness to wholeness. We are vastly different as individuals, but the DNA that makes us all creations of God is exact, and we all share it, just as we all wish to connect on a level higher than we can sometimes explain. We hunger to have a physical encounter with what we cannot see. Worship is our avenue to engage and convey our love for God in limitless, dramatic ways. That connection is created as we express our intimate relationship with our heavenly Father, availing ourselves to the resources available to make worship all that we should desire it to be.

You will be continually amazed how much more is revealed and heightened as your spiritual growth matures and develops in you. This is another phrase that I cannot repeat enough, because the relationship with God is to be inwardly and outwardly renewed and changed. If we start complacently idling where we are because things are good and we feel comfortable, we may stall and never get to experience the best God wants for us. A true worshiper wants to be where God wants her to be; comfortable is unacceptable. Oneness with the Spirit is all that matters.

Several months ago, our family went through the struggle of changing churches, and everything we knew about how to approach the act of worship changed. We noticed that worshiping God was a behavior that was not really understood or pursued by us even though we have been enthusiastic active church-goers for years. Yes, we sang the songs as I mentioned and even felt the emotional beat of the music. Since ancient times, music has played a central role in worship. It is a pivotal force in focusing glory upon God. But during this worship, some element had been missing, making it all seem mechanical.

Unknown to us, we were being prepared to transition from our family's previous place of worship to Keystone Community Fellowship. There seemed to be some sort of undefined turmoil churning in us for some time. Once we deciphered these emotions, we concluded that our hearts were reaching toward God in a deeper way. This was a total God moment for us, because we had been happy, secure, and not looking for any change to disrupt our ordered way of attending church. But one Sunday, a young man showed up at our church and displayed an example of a heart of worship in his countenance. As my husband and I listened and watched him during his musical performance, we could only stare as he sang for an audience of One. Eyes focused on the heavens, his voice was lifted in praise and as an offering of sincere love. God spoke to our hearts that day and strengthened our resolve that proper worship is vital. It was so much more than the music that reached us – anyone can work toward developing a skill, but not many master it in their life. The music was so pure, because it stayed true to the calling God placed on a heart of music, and it sung to the Rock of salvation in spirit and truth. The conversation at home that day led us to the realization that we couldn't deny what was revealed to us through worship. Such adoration for God and His Holy Spirit needed to be placed in our lives and introduced to our children!

At Keystone Community Fellowship we have been blessed with the ministry of worship they provide. Communion, fellowship, and frequent sharing of Christ's love were spread through the music and messages. Having seen everything from music played on the instruments to the awesome singing and praying; we have been amazed at the level of faith that is shared by the unashamed faithful. What a treasure it is to encounter worship that doesn't apologize for its boldness. Every single face shines with the peace of God, because these people have brought themselves and their hearts as a gift before God. Since our family has been partnering in a new way of sharing our faith, we have been introduced to the need to be in front of God, one on one, giving Him all access to our hearts. It is no longer ritual for us when we are in front of God naked and exposed for Him to see all of us. Religion tells us to cover up and act right, as only the elite may enter. Jesus dismisses that thinking and says that the least will be first in His kingdom, and the hurting, lost, and lonely ones matter and have value. Anyone with a heart to believe in Him is welcome! Matthew 20:15-16 says, "...Should you be angry because I am kind? And so it is, that many who are first now will be last then; and those who are last now will be first then." A love so big can only be communicated back in a heart that overflows in praise.

I use the example of the people of our community church to illustrate the point of seeking the form of worship that works for you and helps you express the deepest gratitude of your spirit. There are many styles for worship; we have a Creator of diversity, and we are encouraged to find the way that speaks to you and brings you alive with excited passion for the majestic King above all kings. We as worshipers are free to use whatever motivates our hearts to be captivated beyond just hearing the music in order to produce the exchange and flow of fellowship.

During times of worship, the thought that should be at the center of our minds is the remembrance that the Lord alone deserves the full attention of our hearts. Let these words from the book of Psalms be your reminder each time you want to enter the gates of God's presence through the wonderful sound of unstoppable worship. "The Lord is King! Let the nations tremble! He sits on the throne between cherubim. Let the whole earth quake! The Lord sits in majesty in Jerusalem, supreme above all nations. Let them praise your great and awesome name. Your name is holy! Mighty king, lover of justice, you have established fairness. You have acted with justice and righteousness through Israel. Exalt the Lord your God! Bow low before his feet, for he is holy! (Psalm 99:1-5)

Questions from the Heart

- How would you describe worship? Is what you offer to God based on your reading of John 4:23-24?

- Go back to Psalm 99, which was discussed in the chapter. List the reasons why only the one true God is worthy of our worship. Are there other things taking His place of adoration in your life?

- Most worship songs come right out of the Book of Psalms. Can you find another psalm you think could become a great worship song? What makes it significant to you?

- Are you intimidated when you worship? Do you hold back your emotions because people are watching, or do you come just as you are before God?

- Do you have the heart of worship? Do you express the truth of your heart and accept that Jesus has made us free to dance and sing to Him?

Scripture to Rejoice in

Psalms 107:9 and 92:2, 1 Timothy 4:4, Colossians 3:15, Isaiah 26:3, Romans 15:5-6
Acts 2:42-47, 1 Chronicles 6:31-32, Revelation 4:8-11, Exodus 20:3, Matthew 2:11

Heart Reflections

Heart Reflections

Chapter Four:

Believing the Power of Prayer

A Piece of God's Word – As we know Jesus better, His divine power gives us everything we need for living a godly life. He has called us to receive His own glory and goodness.... So make every effort to apply the benefits of these promises to your life. Then your faith will produce a life of moral excellence. A life of moral excellence leads to knowing God better.... The more you grow like this, the more you will become productive and useful in your knowledge of our Lord Jesus Christ. But those who fail to develop these virtues are blind or, at least, very shortsighted. – 2 Peter 1:3, 5, 8-9

Have no doubt about it; prayer is the only avenue through which you and I will get to know Jesus better. When we pray believing that God will do what He has promised, our faith is built up and the quality of our lives improves. Moral excellence is not achieved by being perfect, but by believing in Jesus as the spiritual compass that guides and directs the decisions we make. Will we follow and apply the Word of God in our lives, or will we be influenced by the world? The power of Christ in us makes us strong when we are weak. When it's dark He will shine His light on us, and when we are hurt He will be our source of strength as we continue to fight and trust that we will see His goodness.

God does not penalize us for faith sometimes having to be grown in us; patience is part of His nature. Of course it is not easy to believe something without proof. Have you heard the phrase, "doubting Thomas"? This phrase comes from a story found in the gospel of John in the familiar dialogue between Jesus and his disciple Thomas. Thomas was not there the first time Jesus showed Himself to the other disciples after His resurrection. Thomas refused to believe the encounter happened until he could see what they had seen. This unbeliever needed to touch the scars of Jesus and placed his finger on His pierced side before he was convinced. (John 20:25-26) The story continues a week later, when Jesus appeared again, this time to Thomas. Then he said to Thomas, "Put your fingers here, and look at my hands; then reach out your hand and put it in my side. Stop your doubting, and believe!"…Jesus said to him, "Do you believe because you see me? How happy are those who believe without seeing me?" (John 20:27-29).

We either simply believe Jesus to be who He is or live waiting for proof that He exists. In order to maintain belief, we need to have a clear focus when we talk to God. Unless we pray in faith, expecting Jesus to intercede on our behalf, we have failed to believe in Him at all. What do we need to believe? I found the following passage compelling because it illustrates the importance of strong faith: "To have faith is to be sure of the things we hope for; to be certain of the things we cannot see. It was by their faith that people of ancient times won God's approval. It is by faith that we understand that the universe was created by God's word, so that what can be seen was made out of what cannot be seen.... No one can please God without faith, for whoever comes to God must have faith that God exits and rewards those who seek him." (Hebrews 11:1-3&6, Good News Version of the Bible)

Tom's Story

My husband has shared with me many stories that helped strengthen his faith. His earliest personal memory about praying and the power of believing in prayer was when he was around age six or seven. I call this "Tom's story," because it is told from the eyes of this child.

Growing up, there was not a time when Tom was a stranger to prayer. Prayer was a high priority in the small country home where he and his nine siblings were raised, led by a mother committed to raising everyone with the principles of praise and prayer. This particular experience from Tom's childhood made a lasting impression upon him and taught him a valuable lesson about God's timing.

It was summer, and the house was charged with anticipation of going on vacation! Curious to see the Winnebago that his dad had rented for their trip, Tom took off out the front door. The front door was just inches from the road, and it was not unusual for the three youngest boys, including Tom, to make a straight break across the street into the neighbor's driveway. Even though this was routine, on this particular day the unfortunate happened. As Tom sped outside, he tripped and took a terrible fall in the road, tearing up his knee.

After his mother picked him up and carried him to the couch, the assessment of Tom's knee was not good. Luckily, a friend of the family who was a nurse happened to be visiting, and she concluded that the family should seriously consider visiting the emergency room. Tom described his knee thus, "Blood was everywhere, stones were embedded inside, and the skin was rolled down past the knee resembling chewed meat!" Nice, huh?

Tom begged not to go to the hospital because stitches would ruin the whole trip! As a young boy, the fear that he might not be able to participate in the family vacation activities kept the tears flowing! Once his mother cleaned out his knee, she laid a much calmer Tom on the parents' bed. The two of them alone prayed together, asking for God's healing. Tom's mother told her son before they prayed that he must believe that Jesus would heal him and then be willing to wait for the blessing. In agreement, they laid their hands on the open wound and prayed. Tom was then given a plain nightstand clock to hold. His mother's instructions were, "You will be healed; now watch this clock and wait on the Lord." She left the room to continue tending to the preparations for the trip. Tom thought about the scripture they had referenced for healing, Matthew 21:21, which says, "I assure you, if you have faith and don't doubt, you can do things like this."

Outside the window near the bed, Tom heard banging of camping gear being loaded, screams of excitement, and the bellow of orders being dispersed between members of the family. Occasionally, someone would pop their head in to give a brief update or to see how Tom was feeling. He held that clock for an hour and a half, praying earnestly that Jesus would heal his knee so that he would be spared from a visit to the hospital and stitches. His heart was fixed on having fun and not missing out on anything. Soon he felt compelled to take a peek, and bravely, Tom looked down at his knee for the first time since he had prayed with his mother.

The description was different this time! Tom's smile while recounting the scene reveals that he still carries the moment with him (as well as a nice scar). When he looked down, the blood had stop completely, the skin had relaxed and rolled back over the knee, and the redness was gone. All that was left was a small line where the skin had been separated and ripped open. He yelled for his mother and family, and they rejoiced together that Jesus brought healing to him, and it appeared that the trip would not be interrupted. The last thing left to do was to treat and apply bandaging to the almost invisible cut, but before any of that was done, God was given thanks and glory for being there and answering their prayer.

It may not be the most dramatic story told, as other people are often healed from worse injuries than that. However, God does all His work in someone's life on the inside first. A gracious, loving God removed any doubt in this family that He is real. Today, as a man, Tom knows that God can be depended on to show up whenever he needs Him. Our marriage has been a testimony to that. In the more than nineteen years we have been married, we have struggled financially because Tom's jobs have always been seasonal and weather permitting. The winters are especially hard economically for us, but each spring Tom continues to smile at me with those sparkling blue eyes that I love, and say, "God has been good, we are still here." Despite the unsteady employment, we made the choice for me to stay home and sacrifice a more glamorous lifestyle so that I could be home to raise our three children. That has been another test we have been given. Even when it seemed like I should get a job too, Tom would remind me to remain faithful and that we would get through. There has been no blessing greater than my ability to be part of every minute of those precious years with my babies.

One of Tom's favorite sayings when things get hard for us is, "Well, I know God will not drop us any further than to our knees." I think that God may have called him on that statement a few times, but never more than when Tom took over when I got sick. Several years ago, I began a downward spiral from an eating disorder. The years of traumatic issues that followed plagued our home and family. Tom watched as my addiction almost led to my destruction. Realizing that he could not handle this situation on his own, once again Tom found himself on his knees in prayer. God answered his prayers because Tom gave over everything to Him, including me, the children, and himself. Tom was given the courage to step up and confront me, compelling me to turn back to God, seek help, and get well. Since then, our home was literally redeemed and our lives have been restored. Everything that happened to heal our home came through the faith of a man's prayers and the grace of God. I thank God every day for my husband, the boy with such faith who grew into a wonderful, God-fearing man. Tom and I have both experienced the growing pains that come with age, the trials of life, and maturity from the hard lessons that had to be learned. We both agree that prayer is what has brought us to where we are today. Our marriage is now stronger than ever because we set our priorities on loving

God first. Since we have received that love back from Jesus, we have the freedom to love each other as God sees us. Love never counts wrongs or sits in judgment; love waits to be there for the other person.

The faith Tom shares with me and with our three children is strong. He hardly would have expected that the lesson he received over thirty years ago could be shared to encourage many others who doubt answers when they pray. God used a little boy whose only prayer was not to have to receive stitches so he could swim to become a man who knows that when we wait for the power of God to come into our lives, great and unimaginable things are given. What also stayed with Tom and brought him great understanding was witnessing through his mother's example that when we pray for or with other people, our belief in what we are praying for makes all the difference to God. Believe in your prayers, but above all, believe first and always in Jesus.

Questions from the Heart

- Do you relate with doubting Thomas in the Biblical story told in this chapter? What do you think you could do to overcome this feeling? (John 20:25-29)

- Is there a story from your life in which prayer was the only thing you could do or hold on to? How has that experience impacted your view on believing in prayer?

- Do you keep a prayer journal or list? If you do, are you willing to share with others how this has been a benefit to you.

- Hebrews 11:1-3 & 6 speaks of the kind of faith we should have. Read this out loud and list anything that is insightful for you to use. Are there also things that can be worked on in your life as you build your faith with the knowledge of Jesus?

- Read the story of mustard seed faith in the gospel of Mark (Mark 4:30-34).What do you get out of this story as it pertains to the amount of faith we need to have?

Scripture to Rejoice in

Mark 5:28-29, Luke 13:24-25, Acts 3:19-20, Hebrews 11, Psalms 26:2-3
Proverbs 4:10-13, 21-23, 25-26, Jeremiah 3:21-22, Matthew 22:37-38, Hosea 2:19

Heart Reflections

Heart Reflections

Chapter Five:

Singing the Songs of Prayer

A Piece of God's Word – "Study this book of law continually. Mediate on it day and night so you may be sure to obey all that is written in it. Only then will you succeed." – Joshua 1:8

For me it has been an amazing experience to study the scriptures and learn that our all-remarkable Creator actually indeed wants to communicate with us. We are creatures of this world who relate to our surroundings through the use of our five senses. The difference between us and God is that we are physical and material beings, and God is a spiritual being. In our physical state, we cannot hear, see, or touch Him, so how is it possible for us to communicate with each other? A way to speak to Him is through prayer, and we can receive communication from him through the Bible. It took several centuries for God to inspire those He called to put on paper the entirety of what He wanted us to know about Him. Even more importantly, these are things that God doesn't merely want us to know, these are the things about Him that He expects us to know. These are not God's feelings or suggestions for us to consider, but His law that we must live. The Bible is called holy because it contains the sacred revelations from an almighty God. In a miraculous way, if you hunger for these secrets, the Bible will reveal them openly and speak to any who seek answers. This book has spoken truth across generations, cultures, and life experiences.

Whenever we purchase a computer, major appliance, or vehicle, we also receive a thick owner's manual with it. I must admit that I usually read just enough out of the manual to learn how to perform the basic tasks of the product. Although many people also try to avoid the boredom of technical reading, do we not equip ourselves with the amount of understanding needed to become capable users of the device we are attempting to master? Most of us will rarely invest the time for sufficient research, so we miss out on all the benefits that are available to us through the gadget we have purchased. When it comes to reading the Bible, we often approach it in the same disinterested way. We want to know what is contained inside and we desire the blessings and the promises we hear it holds, but many of us will do the minimum to get by. We miss much that God's Word has to offer. It sometimes is a challenge for us to read God's Word daily so we can thoroughly understand all the Holy Spirit of God wants us to know. However, I can testify that since I have been centered on consistent Bible reading, it has not only been a delightful discovery of the spiritual as opposed to the carnal but it has also taught me to live for eternity through my receptiveness to the following standards:

1. Blessings come from applying God's Word (Luke 11:28)

2. All Scripture is inspired by God (2 Timothy 3:16)

3. God will help you understand His Word (Hebrews 8:10)

By first understanding these principles, we have laid a foundation of understanding the importance of learning from the Bible. Next let's explore why we have it and why we must use it. We can then move on to realize how the Bible can enhance our lives, much like the appliances we rely on every day. We take for granted the use of many things that we consider vital such as Facebook, Myspace, cell phones, iPods, Blackberries, and endless television channels. These are just a few elements that we let invade our lives and steal our time which we all complain we are short of. Time is better spent devoted to our family, to the community, and foremost to God. I am not waging war on these luxuries of convenience; I am issuing caution. We must take inventory of our current values if we intend to achieve a life lived by godly values. The only place these values are found is in the Holy Bible, still the single manual available today that is never outdated because it explains the character of God and the people who are truly His.

Using the Book of Psalms as a Song Sheet

The Old Testament book of Psalms can be easily used as a manual on its own. Found among the pages of these writings, are words describing every type of prayer we could take to God. We can put our prayers to music and song to capture our feelings of grateful praise because the Bible was penned by men who were in the presence of God; not always physically but definitely always in spirit. The motive of communicating thoughts to God and waiting for a response of action is what implements the elements of prayer. No stronger prayers are created than those uttered during the desperate times of our pain or at the heights of our indescribable joy. As we brush the surface of this powerhouse of a worship book, we will see that God did not leave us unprepared to build a relationship with Him. He gave us the precious words we can use to speak and sing directly to Him! Does that not generate confidence? We have been provided with all we could possibly need to approach God in prayer; even the words have been supplied. Isaiah 8:16 reads, "I will write down all these things as a testimony of what the Lord will do. I will entrust it to my disciples, who will pass it down to future generations." As the word of God becomes life changing for us, we can then pass it on to others, who might experience change in their lives also, the change that being a friend to God always brings.

Many of us have trouble with the rush of our busy lives and do not give life's grander picture even a fleeting glimpse. The range of human emotions a body and mind deal with in a 24-hour period is staggering. How can we possibly be expected to cope with all that is going on inside us? Let's be honest, sometimes we can't. God in His infinite wisdom knew we needed a book in the Bible like Psalms.

Psalms quickly becomes a favorite book for many believers, because it expresses those emotions at the root of our deepest feelings. The candor it includes reaches to the depths of the soul and is wonderfully refreshing.

The psalmists' words help us work through our negative circumstances and understand how to use them to work toward positive service to God. Because a lot of these emotions stem from our sinful nature, we are warned to recognize when evil danger is crossing our path and that it must be avoided at all cost. The psalms teach us that we don't have to hide our feelings; in fact, God encourages us to share them and talk to Him. He wants to talk us through our troubles, anger, pain, frustration, and failures as well as our joys and triumphs. In this exchange of intimate friendship, we begin to know the mind of God. Our hearts will not be able to contain our praise to our Creator for making us responsive to all that goes on around us. Sing songs of praise as you discover and appreciate all the incredible ranges of emotion alive in you. Remember that the ultimate goal to be obtained from each of the 150 psalms is to praise the God who created us in every situation we are in.

As we begin to think of this unique book of scripture as the worship book of prayer and praise, we allow the collection of poems to help us better approach God. Most of the psalms were originally set to music and were intended to be sung. This compilation of writings spanned at least 1,500 years and was made a book of hymns. God loves to hear our voices lifted and filled with song! People are inspired to sing because we have been given an outline directing us to understand everything God does for the ones who call Him Lord. The message delivered through the psalms is the assurance that God comes to us just as we are. He calls us walk near Him and exalt Him as the Lord we follow.

Our challenge is to get to know these songs to God's

heart. There are many psalms that ring familiar to many. We often refer to Psalm 23 as the shepherd's psalm, Psalm 91 is used as a shield of protection when we face fear, and Psalm 139 shows the depths of the creativity God incorporated when He formed each person as a unique masterpiece of His artistry. By acquainting ourselves with the promises of joy contained here, it becomes possible for our weary souls to soar again. These psalms are meant to entice us to continue on and gather what we should reap. The information therein is invitational as always in approaching the wide variety of ideas God's word holds and how we can practically make it relevant in our lives. Once our effort is made to encounter God, we are no longer novices of His ways as the song of salvation and the discovery of deliverance is forever placed in our hearts! Shout with joy to the Lord, O earth! Worship the Lord with gladness. Come before him, singing with joy. Acknowledge that the Lord is God! He made us, and we are his. We are his people, the sheep of his pasture. (Psalm 100:1-3)

Several authors contributed their personal life lessons in this book, including David, Moses, Solomon, Asaph, Korah, Heman, and Ethan. These men were all different in time, age, culture, and background, but they all shared one purpose: to cry out to God through the prayers held in their songs stating that the Lord Almighty was the captor of their hearts! Even a great king such as David honored God and sought His favor. Psalm 103 is King David's own words, pondering the merciful, gracious, and unfailing love that he has seen.

Praise the Lord, I tell myself; with my whole heart, I will praise his holy name. Praise the Lord, I tell myself, and never forget the good things he does for me. He forgives all my sins and heals my diseases. He ransoms me from death and surrounds me with love and tender mercies. He fills my life with good things. My youth is renewed like the eagle's! ...The Lord is merciful and gracious; he is slow to get angry and full of unfailing love.... For his unfailing love towards those who fear him is as great as the heights of the heavens above the earth. (Psalms 103:1-5, 8 & 11)

Close your eyes and see if you cannot hear the song of a perfect prayer.

Questions from the Heart

- What Psalms are you familiar with? What meaning do they hold in your heart?

- Have you ever prayed with a psalm? God loves to hear His words said back to Him. Go to Psalm 102, read it out loud, and list the things that make this a good prayer.

- What are some of the issues of life that you think the book of Psalms gives us insight into? Do you find any comfort or help in the advice from the Psalms?

- What do you think the authors of this book wanted us to understand about God? How would you go about gaining this deeper understanding for yourself?

- Read Psalm 23 and write out all the things that God is to us and provides for us. If something else is revealed to you during this exercise, why not write that down too?

Scripture to Rejoice in

Ezekiel 16:6-7, Micah 6:3-4, Matthew 8:13, Acts 17:11-12, Psalms 1:3, Deuteronomy 32:15-21, Exodus 3:5-6, Joshua 14:10-11, Isaiah 54:6-7

Heart Reflections

Heart Reflections

Chapter Six:

Stages of a Prayer Life

A Piece of God's Word – And I am sure that God, who began a good work within you, will continue His work until it is finished." – Philippians 1:6

As the saying goes, "Rome was not built in day." In the same respect, a prayer life is also formed over a long period of time. Sometimes we strangle our spiritual growth because we tend to get frustrated with believing that we have to become "Super Christians" over night. This is an expectation that we yoke upon ourselves and was never God's intention. God is concerned only about us just speaking to Him. He is not worried about what we still have left to do; only to embrace and rejoice in what has already been done. If all that has been done in your life so far is accepting the salvation of Jesus, then you have already set the perfect stage to begin building an intimate prayer life. A prayer life's first stage is staying in constant communication with our heavenly Father so that nothing interrupts the flow of love between us. Wisdom is the biggest benefit we inherit if we willingly listen to the council of God and open every room of our hearts to Jesus.

In order to succeed in a fruitful prayer life, we need to understand that it is now the Holy Spirit living on the inside of us that makes the things on the outside change. Often, it is the things done on the outside to make the inward change, but prayer is the reverse. Prayer is what we do on the inside with our hearts and minds which reflect out to the world the existence of Christ in our lives. As we go deeper into prayer we develop through different stages; it will become a natural response to ask God for guidance and wait for His direction and leading before we act on our own thoughts. This maturing of our spiritual walk is written about in the book of Hebrews. Let's share this reading together. Solid food is for those who are mature, who have trained themselves to recognize the difference between right and wrong and then to do what is right.

(Hebrews 5:14) So let us stop going over the basics of Christianity again and again. Let us go on instead and become mature in our understanding. And so, God willing, we will move forward to further understanding. (Hebrews 6:1 & 3) It is my belief from these words that gaining knowledge and being faithful in unwavering devotion to God, we will experience the blessing of abundant spiritual growth as our prayers soar to the heart of God.

The Bible verse quoted from Philippians 1:6 says that a good work has been started in all of us. Hear this again, God has began His good work in us with a promise of continuing for however long it takes to get the job done. The job that is being referred to as we read on in the scripture is living our lives with the desire to transform to His image. God's hand remains upon us as we develop until our earthly time is finished, and we begin again new in His Kingdom. Concerning ourselves too much with where we are at in our journey, as compared to others, will distract us from knowing the joy of spending time with Jesus. That place is where we are entirely welcomed and totally secure to be ourselves. The evidence that our prayer life is elevating is seeing the fruit of the Holy Spirit ripen and displayed in us. Galatians 5:22-23 is the well used verse given to us as the marker which examines where our Christian life stands. But when the Holy Spirit controls our lives, he will produce this kind of fruit in us: love, joy, peace, patience, kindness, goodness, faithfulness, gentleness, and self-control. Here there is no conflict with the law. Even if the verse is committed to memory, it must be pulled out often to remind us to keep on going forward.

A dedication to a rich prayer life will stem from our reaction to the following words: "And now we know." How many of us considered talking to God before we knew Him? Do we not need some type of convincing or assurance that there would be a reply to our plight? For some people, the answer is yes. God is okay with us getting to know Him before interacting with Him, but He then tells us to trust that He will do exactly all He claims, "I will open the windows of heaven for you. I will pour out a blessing so great you won't have room enough to take it in! Try it! Let me prove it to you... says the Lord Almighty." (Malachi 3:10) God is a being of unique vision in His measure of time; one day is like a thousand years and a thousand years is like one day. He is not slow in moving, as we define slowness, but patient, granting us ample time to realize we are merely stumbling through our routines without Him. What our heavenly Father wants is for all

His children to come home to be with Him. The one thing God will not do is mess with our free will, so He waits and allows us opportunities in our lives to choose who truly controls our heart.

I think the best evidence to support the statement we are discussing is seen in the gospel of Luke when Jesus hung between two thieves. One of the thieves on Jesus' side had only had a single dialogue with God, which brought Him into the paradise of eternity. It was not the length of His prayer but it was the fact that he could now say that He knew the Son of God and spoke to Him! That momentary conversation brought a broken-hearted man to what it takes some of us a lifetime to reach – repentance. Instantly he moved past the inevitable death of his body and into everlasting life of his soul. Amazing! We will never know the name of that thief, but Jesus did, and so did the angels as they wrote it in the Book of Life. In Luke chapter 23, pay close attention to how quickly Jesus hears our words. In verse 39, one of the criminals hanging on the cross beside Jesus scoffed, "So, you're the Messiah, are you?" Prove it by saving yourself – and us, too, while you're at it." But the other criminal protested, "Don't you fear God even while you are dying? We deserve to die for our evil deeds, but this man hasn't done anything wrong." Then he said, "Jesus, remember me when you come into your Kingdom." The story concludes in verse 43 with Jesus saying, "I assure you, today you will be with me in paradise."

The one thief requested, "Jesus remember me" and God gave His answer through His Son, "You will be with me in paradise." Why? Because all there is to a prayer is a soul giving God the control to work in and through our lives so that we are brought out of this world to His Kingdom in paradise. Both of the thieves next to Jesus were offered the chance to be with Him, and until that point nothing they did in their lives mattered as much as that moment of decision. So what are we doing? Are we scoffing at Jesus, waiting for proof that He can save us from our sin? Or will we turn to face Him now and ask that He remember us from this minute on as a new creation ready to be with Him? The man who went to heaven did not have a chance to live out what Jesus did for Him here on earth, but he was loved enough to be able to rejoice for eternity because he seized the moment out of death.

One Love: Terry & Beth's example

I am blessed to have been in rich supply of sisters and sisters-in-law. Witnessing Christ in so many of the women in my family is a rare treasure. Each of us has a unique approach in our marriages, child-rearing philosophies, career choices, and type of church we attend, but we have the salvation of Jesus as our common tie and His commands are the codes we all strive to live by.

This story of the practical living of scripture, presents both my sister Beth, and my sister-in-law Terry. These women are at different ends of the spectrum with regard to the stages they have achieved in their prayer life. One has made a nearly twenty-one year commitment to raise her children, conduct her marriage, and run her home under the authority of God; the other has experienced a recent conversion that has brought peace, love, and clarity to her life. Did one of them do it better than the other? I think that I will agree with God when He says the only thing that matters is that each soul is made right with

Him when we believe in Jesus. Since we have been made right in God's sight by faith, we have peace with God… (Romans 5:1-2) What we need in order to be "doing it right" is obtaining that salvation in lives of virtue, service, and peace within our spirit.

Terry has raised her nine children on the foundation of Godly principles. Her motto, which was used often while raising these babies, was, "Teach your children to choose the right path, and when they are older, they will remain upon it." (Proverbs 22:6) She took the responsibility from that verse to engage in prayer early in each child's life, and now as her older children are becoming young adults, she is reaping the fruition of this promise. Terry relied on prayer through the seasons of growth, holding strong to her convictions from her first child on through the last. Of course she has learned a lot and possibly changed how she has done things over the years, as all parents do, but her practice of introducing God to her children never changed. They were all raised the same way, talking to God, thanking God, and asking others and God to forgive them. If one commits to a practice long enough, it seems to become part of us, and I think that is how it has been for Terry; she wanted God's presence in every stage. Not long ago, she and I had a conversation about being mothers of teenage daughters and sons, and she said, "You know, I have been praying for many years and my prayer still remains, "Lord make me the mother my children need me to be." She made me think that the good work done in the early stages of our walk with God will continue as we look forward to what God wants each one of us to be as His beloved child!

My sister Beth's experience has been a little different.

She has recently given her life to the Lord and is at the beginning of her exploration of the gift that a new way of life has to offer. I love the phone calls, emails, inspiring articles, and text messages she sends me. What I love even more is sharing the joy found in the Lord with my sister. Everything that seems so fresh to her is becoming fresh again to me. Her excitement for Jesus is contagious. Her eyes are seeing the truth in what she never understood before, and one revelation that she has received is how close God is when we pray.

One day we were all attending an anniversary party for our parents. Beth had driven the distance from Pennsylvania to Maryland alone with her six-year-old son. After saying hello, she began eagerly telling me a story. The smile she had on her face was as bright as the sun as she recalled her morning. Before the car left the driveway, Beth introduced prayer for the first time to her son, Alex. As they folded their hands, Alex became nervous about what they were doing. His mother told him that they were going to ask God to keep them safe and bless their trip. When they pulled up to the restaurant where the party was, they thanked God for hearing their prayers.

The next day Beth called me with another story about prayer. Long car rides are hard for my sister, so they spent the night at our mother's home in Maryland after the party. The ride home was a traveler's nightmare; nothing was going right. Beth and Alex got lost and were detoured through unfamiliar Philadelphia streets. They eventually ended up in New Jersey, a state they were not intending to be in. Their anxiety rose, and then Alex said something to her. He said, "Mommy, what about this?" and he folded his hands in front of him to show her that he wanted to pray.

To her surprise, she knew what to do; this new Christian was able to take control of their situation. Her prayer to God was this, "Okay God, I am new. I believe you, you got me. Don't let me down. I know this is a test and I want to pass it. Get us home safely and keep us calm." After that point she pulled over to get something to eat and had a wonderful lunch with her son. The rest of the trip home was long, and the poor child wanted nothing more to do with freeways, but they pulled into their driveway seven hours later (our mother lives only three hours away!) safely and having taken their level of prayer to the next stage.

If I had to pick a verse that would capture Beth's motto, it would be Psalms 17:15; "But because I have done what is right, I will see you. When I awake, I will be fully satisfied, for I will see you face to face." Beth, her husband, and their two children are growing closer to God in faith each day. Now that they have gone from the point of having no relationship with the Lord to praying for salvation, this family is on the path to eternity. The children love church, and the parents are experiencing another stage of their marriage together as they connect more deeply with a Christ-centered approach to life.

The past paths of these two women may not be equal, between they are the same in the sight of God, because He is involved and included in their lives. All God requires is that a life be lived on the E.D.G.E. – Experiencing, Discovering God Everywhere.

Questions from the Heart

- Do you get frustrated because you look at some people and think that they are living life better than you are? As you study the verses shared throughout this chapter, record your feelings and promptings from God.

- Write about your first experience when you asked Jesus into your heart with prayer. Do you remember what it meant to you and if that time brought you to a more spiritual level when you talked to God?

- Based on the following verse from Psalms, do you think it matters more to God when we start our relationship & prayer life or do you think He just wants us to start?

Psalms 18:19-20
...But the Lord upheld me. He led me to a place of safety; He rescued me because he delights in me. The Lord rewarded me for doing right; He compensated me because of my innocence.

- Revisit Luke 23:39-43. When you hear that a thief was admitted into heaven minutes before death, what thoughts come to your mind? How do you feel about that?

- Read over the words in that same passage in Luke; put yourself in both places. Consider the situation from the perspective of Jesus hanging on a cross, seeing someone God loves. Then consider it from the eyes of the thief, someone who has never known God's love until that moment. See if your answers to the last two questions agree or if you have been shown something different with these two perspectives.

Scripture to Rejoice in

Matthew 7:7, Ephesians 3:2-7, Psalms 38:15-18, James 1:5 & 5:16, 1 John 5:14,
2 Corinthians 12:7-10, Isaiah 1:16-20, Nehemiah 2:4, Deuteronomy 4:29, Acts 11:18

Heart Reflections

Heart Reflections

Chapter Seven:

Turning Prayer into a Poem

A Piece of God's Word – "Yes, there will be an abundance of flowers and singing and joy! The deserts will become green as the mountains of Lebanon, as lovely as Mount Carmel's pastures and the Plain of Sharon. There the Lord will display his glory, the splendor of our God."
– Isaiah 35:2

Have you ever meditated upon the splendor of our God? Isaiah the prophet paints an exquisite picture of Jesus our Messiah and His everlasting Kingdom, which is to come. The beauty in Isaiah's words beckons to us to abandon everything that is sinful and turn to God. At the time of this writing, Jesus had not yet been born, so like the people Isaiah preached to, we also must hold on to future joys and blessings and believe in what God is preparing to happen. Isaiah is the book in the Old Testament that speaks to the Jewish people about the coming Savior, a prelude to the coming of Jesus Christ.

The passage written in Isaiah 35:2 offers hope for restoration in our lives because of the excellence of God.

Read how alive the verse is in its description of nature. The brilliance of the earth is portrayed as an empty canvas coming alive with each stroke of God's artistry. The atmosphere just seems filled with nature's music. Are you not sometimes stunned by the masterpiece of creation? The excellence that God creates is more than a routine task or an object that was made out of necessity alone; it flows from His hand in abundance, beauty, and harmony. God involves us as well; He wants you and me to participate in how we think and work and even how we talk to Him. God gave us life and everything in it to be used, enjoyed, and blended together for His glory to be displayed as majestically excellent for all to witness. These beautiful images of perfection inspire us all to stay focused upon seeking justice, righteousness, and salvation; because these are the great things we want to experience flourishing in our lives. The beauty of God's wonder invites us to draw creatively closer into a spiritual life with grand expectation.

Through the re-told stories of the scriptures, God displays his passion for beauty and speaks to us in various ways. Rainbows appear, thunderstorms arise, the earth quakes, and stars dazzle the night sky, representing just a few methods that God uses to get our attention in a way we understand – visual. When our hearts and minds are so full of our own lives, then the overflow of creativity is poured out through us as well. Psalm 45:1 says, "My heart overflows with a beautiful thought! I will recite a lovely poem to the king, for my tongue is like the pen of a skillful poet."

Did you know that we can pray to God with creativity? Creativity is all about uniqueness, whether it is fashioning something, shaping a thought, or conceiving a new approach to what it is you are doing. We admire it, copy it, and are enthralled when we can exercise it. God has already been established in the studies that are shared as the greatest example for our personal creativity, because we see how wildly creative He was in making our world. The Bible shows us many places in which creativity can be used in enhancing any area. Even when we are alone in prayer with God, we can be creative in the way we allow the Holy Spirit to recreate us. God's spirit is what inwardly transforms us and releases us in freedom to be who we were designed to be. It would be impossible to list all the ways that creativity can be expressed. God's creative works are an example for us to use in our spiritual journey as we begin exploring creative ways to glorify and praise Him.

I want to touch on prayer as a way to open yourself to God in the most natural demonstrations that seem proper to you. The other "how-to" recommendations for a prayer life are things most of us understand. What is important for us to know is that we can have a conversation with God that brings us comfort and inner peace with our Creator. It is a wonderful transition from our temporary problems into meditation upon the promises of eternal hope in our Redeemer. If you gain the ability to transport your mind, body, and soul into the presence of God and be with Him, then your prayers have moved from words to poetry. This becomes the point at which your heart is speaking along with your mind. Challenge yourself the next time you are in prayer and attempt one creative way that you can be expressive to God. Creativity in our spirits occurs when we see the barren deserts turn to green mountains and flowers bloom in abundance where before there was nothing. Sing with joy as you pray, knowing the prospect of all the good things through Jesus that God has planned for us long ago.

Caryn's Poem

It has been made openly known that the theme behind the *Mother in Love* series is to share the lessons that have been taught through a godly life – lessons and love that touched more people than we may ever know. The people affected the greatest were the family members. In-laws included, all were embraced without exception with acceptance.

Another of my sisters-in-law, Caryn, and I used to joke with each other. We would tease by saying that one or the other of us is the favorite Mrs. Barrett. It is our inside joke, but we knew how much we have been loved by our mother-in-law. Both of us realized quickly in our married lives how exceptional our mother-in-law was. The reality of her not being here any longer hit us hard when it was time to say goodbye for a time. God blessed us with more than an in-law; He provided a friend.

In the final days before we had to let Mom go, the family followed their own way of processing their reactions. We prayed, sang, talked, and even laughed as we became aware of all that we had been given to us through this one person. I know many of you have had that experience with special people in your life, so you will be able to relate to some of the feelings that we were feeling.

Caryn also had a meaningful relationship with Mom, but her experience as she was praying to God early one morning brought into her heart the awareness that life is bigger than we are; it isn't so much how much time we have, but what we have done with the time God has given us that makes us relevant. She sat quietly praying and asking God to help her get through the loss of a loved one, but she later told me that so much more was happening. Among her sadness, Caryn seemed also to be captivated by the beauty that was around her as she looked at the sunrise and the first glimpse of a new day. The vision really made her heart feel full, and her prayer took a different form than ever before; it became creative.

Her pain was lifted out of her and onto paper, but as the words were written, the pain somehow transformed into thanksgiving and praise for the goodness that God has showed by supplying this person to be in her life for a brief time. I pray that I am relating her encounter with God with sufficient power. It was amazing to me how she described her feelings sitting there meditating upon God and looking at the wonder of His creation while He moved quietly in her heart of prayer to birth a beautiful poem of remembrance.

We don't know for sure, but it comforts us to think that Mom did hear this poem, because as it was read at her bedside, she was already slipping away and could not communicate with us any longer. Her slight smile and eye movements gave us peace that God let her hear it in her own way. I know that it is Caryn's wish to have this poem shared as her tribute to how instrumental and valuable Mom was to her. Her husband Pat read it at the funeral, because Caryn was too overwhelmed to do so, but she stood right next to him and for a moment, I believe she was the favorite Mrs. Barrett, because Mom made each person in her life feel as though they were her favorite.

God is so limitless in what He will do with our

emotions. Every time we give Him our pain, sorrows, or joy, it is an invitation to Him to get creative in His work in our lives. I love just waiting to see what He is going to do when my heart is opened to be reached. Prayer brings us to that place where we can say, "God, I love you, I need you, I can't make it without you." Sometimes when His hand meets ours, it turns into a poem that He helps us write. Here is Caryn's poem, called *The Gift*. Each word that started as a prayer finished as something constructed to shine the glory on God. Read it and enjoy, and remember that artistry and uniqueness were planted inside you.

The Gift
By Caryn Barrett

Thank you for the gift Lord, for it is plain to see
Not everyone in this world has a mother-in-law like me.
Never a correction, never a cross word,
Only smiles with quiet advice, and hugs for boys and girls.
Many a grandchild slept on her, many a baby cried
None of us could ever count how many tears she dried.
Always there to hold someone's hand or even just to sit
She knew when to be serious or charm you with her wit.
Years of memories flood back now,
and these we will tuck away
For they will keep us moving forward,
through all the rainy days
So thank you for the gift Lord, for
in our hearts we'll keep
The memory of the woman, whose love for you runs deep
Amen

Questions from the Heart

- What moves your heart when you're speaking to God? Do you focus on His excellence and beauty, or do you rush to complete the list of things you need done?

- Can you remember a time that you expressed creativity in you prayer life?

- Re-read Isaiah's verse that began this chapter. Note how Isaiah uses colors and the images of nature to describe the work of God. When you think of the brilliance God uses in creation, what words do you use?

- Psalms 45:1 tells us that a beautiful thought will move our thoughts into words of a poem. If this is true for you, will you attempt as Caryn did, putting that beauty into a short poem for God?

- God gives us this challenge in the book of Philippians 4:8: "And now dear brothers and sisters, let me say one more thing before I close this letter. Fix your thoughts on what is true and honorable and right. Think about things that are pure and lovely and admirable. Think about things that are excellent and worthy of praise." Go ahead and mark that verse in your Bible for future reminders! Now read that out loud and make any notes that may help you apply this to the things you spend time thinking about.

Scripture to Rejoice in

Philippians 4:9, Romans 8:39, Song of Songs 7:10 (or Song of Solomon in some versions of the Bible), Deuteronomy 7:9 & 30:20, Genesis 1:31 & 2:1-4, Matthew 25:29 James 5:16, Revelation 22:16, 1 Thessalonians 4: 11-12, Psalms 121:8

Heart Reflections

Heart Reflections

Chapter Eight

What Are You Praying For?

A Piece of God's Word – "But when you pray, go away by yourself, shut the door behind you, and pray to your Father secretly. Then your Father, who knows all secrets, will reward you. When you pray, don't babble on and on as people of other religions do. They think their prayers are answered only by repeating their words again and again. Don't be like them, because your Father knows exactly what you need even before you ask him!" – Matthew 6:6-7

As a new Christian, when I first read those two verses from Matthew, I wondered why Jesus gave us that teaching. If God knows what I need, why am I praying? Then I re-read Matthew 6:5, which reads, "And when you pray do not be like the hypocrites... who love to pray on the street corners... where everyone can see them. I assure you, that is the only reward they will get." Here we are warned to be mindful with our actions and what we do for the Lord. Prayers or service for God is not purposed for a public display intended solely for recognition. Are we like the hypocrites, doing our good acts for rewards? That's a tough question isn't it? From my understanding, most of the things that Jesus requires of those who choose to follow Him are challenging. The four gospels relate numerous stories of how Jesus, the son of a carpenter, asked people to radically change their lives and their views. One major charge Jesus suggested, back in Biblical times and still today, is to keep in check our religious behaviors. We need to ask ourselves frequently, does it make me feel good when people notice what I do? Is it more important for me to convey the appearance of spirituality and talking the talk instead of being concerned about walking the walk? The test of knowing the Holy Spirit comes solely in deciding to live out the principles we talk about, sometimes even when we are alone without an audience.

My question was answered; God does know what we are going to pray for, but He waits for us to bring it to Him because He wants us to know why we are praying and what it is we think we need. Born-again Christians are not kept on a puppet string, being yanked wherever the puppet master forcibly directs without any voice in the performance. Instead of negativity and the heavy-handed grip of strongholds, we enjoy the mercy seat of God, where we are loved and accepted and desired to be close to. We pray because God likes to hear from us and desperately wants to be the one to help us. As we continue to look specifically into these aspects of prayer, our top priority is to communicate with God as we would a best friend; the other is to count on Him to be there to do what is promised. Only those prayers grounded in the deep roots of faith are going to move the seemly impossible obstacles around us and give us the clarity we need to know exactly what it is we are praying for.

The Prayer of Jabez

This is, without a doubt, my favorite prayer ever recorded in the Bible by a man. The only words that compare are the words that Christ prayed as He hung on the cross for the sake of humanity. I am excited to discover with you all that the prayer of Jabez contains. One of the best-known book commentaries written about this passage of the Old Testament is by Bruce Wilkinson, and I can promise you that if you read his small book with an open heart, it will affect how you view what you are praying for. I can add nothing more to the passage, but can only capture some of the meaning that the remarkable prayer of an unfamiliar Bible hero holds for us. There is not much known about Jabez; he is mentioned only one time in the whole Bible in those two verses. What we do know is what he left through his prayer, which has been his legacy. Can it be that easy to unleash God's favor with a few ordinary sentences? How can we be assured of power and protection if we do not spend enough revenant time in prayer stating to God what our needs are? This man named Jabez figured out how to get God's attention and understood what it meant to live the kind of life he was supposed to. Jabez spoke to God and prayed a prayer that broke through the barrier of self, leaving his past behind allowing him to walk ahead with the extravagant grace and blessings of God.

Prepare yourself to be introduced to this small but life-changing message from someone who made God's honor roll boldly thinking, "So, why not ask?" Surely you will want to highlight this passage in your Bibles, but let's read together these words made by a man who was not afraid to stretch to the heavens and ask for blessings.

There was a man named Jabez who was more distinguished than any of his brothers. His mother named him Jabez because his birth had been so painful. He was the one who called on the God of Israel saying, "Oh that You would bless me indeed, and enlarge my territory, that Your hand would be with me, and that You would keep me from evil, that I might not cause pain!" (1 Chronicles 4:9-10)

How could a prayer like that earn compensation from God? Sometimes when I pray I begin to think that the only way for God to understand what I need is to give an analytical explanation of my needs and desires. The example of prayer given by Jabez has made a huge impact on me by reminding me that a prayer needs only to consist of four components:

1. "That You would bless me indeed" – We need to ask God to bless us. The manner in which God will bless our lives and in what areas He chooses to bless us are His concern, but we just need to ask that He grant us His favor where it is best. God's blessings are too many to even mention or attempt to count. They come new to us every day, in every conceivable form. "Blessed are those who trust in the Lord and have made the Lord their hope and confidence" (Jeremiah 17:7)

2. "...enlarge my territory" – This request portrayed a desire for God to provide more than land or livestock and material pleasures. Jabez wanted opportunities to speak to more and more people

about the goodness of God. The territory he was after was the capacity to share salvation. Have we asked God to bring people into our lives that we could possibly influence in a positive way? Jabez seemed to grasp the idea that every believer should be God's ambassadors to a non-believing world. "They will see your honorable behavior and believe" (1 Peter 2:12)

3. "...that Your hand would be with me" – There is nothing specific God is asked to do in this phrase except that He be present in every situation. I think Jabez makes it clear that he simply longs for God to be with Him in whatever he did and wherever he went. I was challenged to think here for a moment and check whether I run ahead of God with my plans or if I ask Him to guide them from the beginning. Asking God to be with you indicates that you want to give Him control, because you trust Him with your life. Seeking and finding God requires purposeful prayer. God said, "When you pray, I will listen... you will find me when you seek me" (Jeremiah 29:11-13)

4. "...that You would keep me from evil, that I might not cause pain." – Does part of this prayer sound familiar? Didn't we hear this somewhere before in the Bible, the plea to be kept out of evil's way? The devil knows where we are weak, and he closes in each time we allow a space to open between ourselves and the Lord. I believe that if we read those few words again it will remind us of the words Jesus said to His disciples as He taught

them how to pray. If we compare the prayer Jesus prayed in Matthew 6:5-13 to the one of Jabez, we find that they are similar in what is asked. Both are prayers requesting provision of daily needs, stating a commitment to obedience to the will of God, and a plea for protection from every type of temptation that creeps into our lives. Exemplified through prayers like these is the intimate relationship with the Father based on our dependency. We need the strength that only the Spirit of God can bring to the things that threaten us that we can't see. God is never tempted to do wrong, and He never tempts anyone else either. (from James 1:12-16)

Jabez hit the bull's eye in his depiction of a prayer life. He did not go on and on with words; he got to the point and waited for God's descending power to come upon his request. I believe that if we conditioned our minds to pray that way every day, we too would see some incredible results. Remember to pray following those four points. Seek blessings, opportunities, obedience, and the protection of God. God's nature is to bless us to the maximum, and through simple believing prayer, you can change your future. There is no way to put boundaries on God; He is unlimited in His resources and willingness to give to us even more than we are able to receive.

We must keep our focus clear when we pray. When we figure out for ourselves the things we ought to being praying for, our needs become secondary and we become immersed in what God is trying to do in us, through us, and for us. This transformation will not be easy if we do not participate, as we often talk about, with God. Finding a quiet place, writing, or walking alone will help build a respective bridge so that we can better share our thoughts with God. An appropriate setting sets the stage for us to move in God's direction without obstructions so that we can pray exactly how God desires.

Is it possible that God wants us to ask for abundance as Jabez did? There may be Christians who would say that this is a sign of a greedy nature, but it is supremely spiritual. God astounds us with His answer to this question. "God has given gifts to each of you… Manage them well so that God's generosity can flow through you" (1 Peter 4:10). God's purpose here is to be good to us so that the more we get and give of ourselves, the more God's generosity flows through us and brings glory to Him. When God answers our prayers, it is a blessing to us so that it can also be passed on to others. The Holy Spirit wants to be a regular part of each day, and God wants to give us far beyond what we have ever thought to ask for. We do not have to live with the spiritual status quo; we can reach for more. God is all about granting us abundance – overflowing and running over with blessings. "For this reason I remind you to fuel the flames of the spiritual gift God gave you… For God has not given us a spirit of fear and timidity but power, love, and self discipline" (2 Timothy 1:6-7).

So many things seem to be done out of repetition; the reason for this is because there are only a few things that God really wants us to understand about Him. He wants us to talk transparently with Him, He wants us to trust Him to be enough for all we need, He wants us to know that Jesus Christ is the way to Him, and He wants us to be good to others so that His love can shine in the world. The question, "What are you praying for?" can be answered through the understanding that God wants to give us the desires of our hearts. "Trust in the Lord and do good. Then you will live safely in the land and prosper. Take delight in the Lord, and he will give you your heart's desires. Commit everything you do to the Lord, and he will help you" (Psalm 37:3-5). He wants His work to be done in each one of us. The answer becomes as individual as we are in that each must ask God to show us what His will for our life is. The following psalm may aide in wrapping up the topic of what should inspire us to pray: "Acknowledge that the Lord is God! He made us, and we are his. We are his people; the sheep of his pasture... For the Lord is good. His unfailing love continues forever, and his faithfulness continues to each generation" (Psalms 100:3 & 5). The prayer given by Jabez sounds like that. Jabez acknowledged God, trusted that God had him in His hands, and knew that God would be good to him.

Finally, Jabez's prayer was simple. He asked for God to be with him and to bless him in everything he did. This was not a prayer to satisfy greed, but an illustration of reliance on God to meet every need. It bears repeating that Jabez did not recite his own prayer request list for each issue he had in his life. He knew that God knew the details. What God seeks from us, like Jabez, is to speak from our heart. With the same plea of Jabez as part of our life, we too can climb to a higher level in honoring God's trustworthy and steadfast character to exponentially expand His blessings. Through Christ we are made alive to live in triumph – not in temptation or defeat. As Mr. Wilkinson points out in his commentary, "What an amazing declaration of victory!" Consider letting God point you in the direction of spiritual success, and spend time practicing this prayer that was answered with supernatural service.

Questions from the Heart

- Has God ever answered something a prayer for something significant? Can you remember and describe in your personal pages how you felt?

- Are you bold in your prayers, like Jabez, knowing that you serve a God who is big and gracious to provide? Can you think of anything holding you back?

- Do you personally view situations as being to big for God to handle or too small for God to care about? Does your answer leave you with the question, "so why pray"?

- Does reading the prayer of Jabez change anything about what you think you should be praying for?

- Go back in the chapter or to your Bible and read the prayer of Jabez out loud. Make a list for yourself outlining what strikes you as to why this was a prayer that God quickly answered.

Scripture to Rejoice in

James 1:5, Galatians 6:9, Revelation 2:3, 1 John 1:9 & 2:6,
2 Thessalonians 3:3
Genesis 50:20, Nehemiah 1:10-11, Zephaniah 3:16-17, 2
Corinthians 5:17 & 6:1-2

Heart Reflections

Heart Reflections

Chapter Nine

Standing Together As Prayer Warriors

A Piece of God's Word – "The harvest is so great, but the workers are so few. So pray to the Lord who is in charge of the harvest; ask him to send out more workers for his fields." – Matthew 9:37-38

We do not often view prayer as work, but praying and interceding for others is exactly what Christians are called to be doing. Prayer is part of our work in God's Kingdom. Jesus saw all people as valuable creations of God in need of healing, encouragement, and salvation; He did not write anybody off; instead He spoke to them about God's love and prayed that their hearts would be changed. During His public ministry, Jesus walked with people, talked with people, and prayed with people. The journey He was on was lived for everyone to be part of. The lifestyle Jesus preached was unity among believers. He knew that if we could not get along with our brothers and sisters we could not be in agreement with God who we cannot yet see. Jesus interceded, becoming the mediator between us and God. He prayed for people, demonstrating the attitude that is to be maintained for us who have a relationship with the Lord. In the gospel of John, Jesus speaks of how His name is to be used as representation in prayer to the Father and our model. In John 16:23-24, Jesus gives us these words, "At that time you won't need to ask me for anything. The truth is, you can go directly to the Father and ask him, and he will grant you your request because you ask in my name. You haven't done this before. Ask, using my name, and you will receive, and you will have abundant joy."

Once again, we see Jesus' final breaths on earth spent for us. As the people stood mocking Him, Jesus hung on the cross, suffering and praying on their behalf. Jesus said, "Father, forgive these people, because they don't know what they are doing." …The crowd watched, and the leaders laughed and scoffed. (Luke 23:34-35) I am convinced that we are called to do no less than to pray for others as Jesus prayed for us. We must pray for those who need the blessings of God poured upon their lives. Jesus is always speaking to God on our behalf until we receive the desire to go to God ourselves. When committed people gather specifically to pray for others, it is something we must witness to be able to describe. I've seen prayer that was so gentle it felt like a rhythmic wave, with everything flowing. I have also been a part of intercessory prayer in which the Sprit was so alive with fire that we believed the gates of hell were being rattled and victory was indeed ours!

Many things were explained to me when I started my journey of salvation. Praying for and with others was one of the earliest lessons I learned. I had the mentoring of my mother-in-law, who patiently invested her time in weaving the lessons of scripture into my life. The "Mother in Love" series has been my way of encapsulating the spiritual teachings and guidance I was given as a new believer and the gentle and loving way it was all introduced. She wanted me, just as is my hope for you, to live a life fully converted out of religion and into relationship with Jesus. My mother-in-law often joked with us about ruining her knees and her chances of looking good in a bathing suit! The amount of time she spent on them in prayer for so many of us made them hard and calloused like a camel's. Those knees may not have been attractive to her, but it was the beauty of the work that God did through them that was all we saw. I strive to make my knees look exactly like that. Time on our knees is time spent with God. It was a good way of putting meaning to the words… "Before we can stand together, we must kneel alone." Please do not misunderstand; the Christian life is not a solitary existence. We are to put hands and feet to the body of Christ, but before we can do that we must face the truth of our hearts before God. Once that happens, we enlist in God's army, preparing to take our place among the ranks and stand together to fight the good fight needed in showing the world the love of Jesus. "The throne of God and the Lamb will be in the city, and his servants will worship him. They will see his face, and his name will be written on their foreheads. There shall be no more night, and they will not need lamps or sunlight, because the Lord God will be their light, and they will rule as kings forever and ever" (Revelation 22:3-5). Imagine being on the side that will not loose.

Mr. and Mrs. Kempf's Story

My life has been blessed with the influence of people who in different ways have portrayed the evidence of a

Christ-centered life. Mr. and Mrs. Kempf is a couple who learned how to stand together in prayer as a team. It was not always a rosy path for them. Mr. Kempf spent years struggling with his own strongholds and addictions of this world. Then one day in the 1970s, he was watching "The 700 Club" with Pat Robertson, when everything began to change for him. He realized his brokenness and need of the salvation of Jesus. He dedicated the rest of his life to the service of God and advancing His kingdom. Mr. Kempf allowed nothing to hold him back, breaking every shackle that held him captive in bondage by the grace of deliverance. The faithfulness of his wife to remain convinced that God would do this for her husband gave testimony to the greatness and power of prayer! Wielding his thick German accent and big, tall frame, he was a force on fire to share the message of the gospel.

The Kempfs and their children are among the family's dearest friends. Both my mother-in-law and Mr. Kempf have left this world to go home and join the great cloud of witnesses that have made it to the heavenly realms. But it is in the legacies of what they accomplished here, that will affect generations still to come. The trio prayer team would not be stopped or kept away from where God told them to go. They prayed over each other's homes, children, grandchildren, great-grandchildren, marriages, businesses, health, finances, and many more aspects. Mrs. Kempf will forever remember the home wedding reception of one of their children. She laughs now about how the food was almost gone, with only four meatballs left and a few other sparse items. There were still numerous people left to feed; some of the people had not even shown up yet. It was also getting late, and food stores were already closing, as ours was not then the 24-hour society it is now. So, Mr. Kempf prayed boldly and quite seriously for God to supply a miracle by multiplying the meatballs like the fishes and loaves and provide enough for the guests. Do I need to tell you that God did exactly that and that at the end of the night there was extra food? It did not surprise God that after everyone was fed they ended up with nine plus the original four meatballs. This is an example of those wonderful things that cannot be explained here. All that can be said is that God showed up when He was called upon. Whenever prayer was used, it was always done with the belief that it was going to be answered."Who can forget the wonders he performs? How gracious and merciful is our Lord! He gives food to those who trust him; he always remembers his covenant" (Psalms 111:4-5).

There was not an area off limits for the Kempfs to try to reach. They often prayed around in the community, even walking through neighborhoods and apartment complexes that were known for trouble. How awesome is the privilege of going out into the places in which we live and praying peace upon people's lives?

But what if God calls us out of the familiar life we know? One undeniable trait of a prayer warrior is that they are on call for others. Our personal burden and personal expense is not counted or considered, but the mission is all about an act of selfless obedience and love for the things of the Holy Spirit. There is a difference between prayer partners and prayer warriors. Prayer partners do intercede for others and their needs in a united front, but prayer warriors involve themselves with the actual people and situations for which they are praying. They walk to the front lines of conflict, prepared to face the attacks that the enemy will fire.

What I found remarkable about the Kempfs in their stand as prayer warriors is that they were called to leave their family, grown children, and home here in America and go off to preach the gospel as missionaries in a foreign land. This was not an easy decision or emotional whim, but a deep calling to travel to all the ends of the world so that the message of God is heard by all people. Much prayer, and listening to the call God placed on their hearts, went into exploring all their options. Finally, they entrusted my in-laws to keep an eye on their loved ones here, as they tackled the difficulties on the mission field in a foreign country. The experiences that Mr. and Mrs. Kempf encountered could fill their own book. What is important to know is the powerful way they witnessed and taught about the love of Christ. They were able to be part of transforming many dark lives into light. These are true prayer warriors on the path, which only goes one way, to God and they did what it took to put others on it by lifting them up to the throne which is in heaven.

Illness bought the Kempfs back to the states for good about four years after their departure, but their mission work was nowhere near over. From 1991 to 1993, they lived back at the mission headquarters and were counselors to Bible students. They remained involved in people's lives, attending Bible studies, church services, and home prayer groups. The meaning of the passage, "Where two or three gather together because they are mine, I am there among them" found in Matthew 18:20 became real for them when they joined a group called Jesus Focus Ministries. In 1976, my mother-in-law had introduced the Kempfs to this place. They were yet unaware how much of themselves would be invested and what would be required of their time, spiritual gifts, and energy. They faithfully attended daily non-denominational Bible classes, and Friday nights were set for prayer and praise. Through these classes, the community gathered and kept their passion for being recruited for Christ refueled.

Being a prayer warrior is a commitment of time. Time, as I shared earlier, is spent both being involved personally with people and sitting in prayer with supplication. Mailings from the ministry were mailed out weekly with prayer requests including situations that would be lifted in prayer for a month. Often, if the situation was serious, Mr. and Mrs. Kempf or my mother-in-law would meet right away with the person as Christian counselors. Sometimes they would spend hours praying with the people and working through an ordeal. Their belief was that you never know whose life you will touch and that you should always be ready to go. Even as I listen to her stories, Mrs. Kempf reaches in her bag and pulls out this week's prayer request from Jesus Focus Ministries, a habit of thirty-three years and counting! The years have not lessened her zeal to fight for the souls the enemy wants to steal. Mrs. Kempf's recent endeavor is serving on staff as a hospice companion where she can offer comfort and dignity during a person's last days. What a fitting tribute to her husband, best friend, and prayer partner that she is continuing to fill the gap for others as she was so committed to do so many years ago.

What can be said to sum up the life of a prayer warrior? When I asked that question to Mrs. Kempf during our conversation, she did not hesitate. She answered, "God calls you to the work and He strengthens you for the task. I don't have to see the results, I just pray when I am called to pray. I may never get to see what God is going to do through someone, but I know He will always do something. All people who believe in prayer must carry the attitude that it is a privilege and honor. Above all, even when the path sometimes beats you down, no matter how tired you get, you only need to pray a prayer as simple as 'Lord please have mercy.'"

It is such a gift to have someone in my life like Mrs. Kempf, who speaks God's Word the way it is. Whenever I need to, I know that I can pick up the phone or go visit her, and she will start praying for whatever the situation may be. She is now one of the first individuals I turn to for spiritual guidance, because her story has proven that she has remained determined to study and obey the law of God. She is faithful in teaching those laws and regulations to those she is in contact with because she lives it daily.

What I really like about a relationship with the Lord is that we do not have to form it all at once. Every promise we read in the Bible tells us that God guides us and lifts us up so that we will remain encouraged to continue to live a changed life. God wants to spend time first speaking with us, healing us, refreshing us, and strengthening us before He sends us out into service. Does that mean God can't use us as we are learning? On the contrary; He absolutely can. Think about those entering basic training in the armed forces. The trainees are not given their weapons on the first day or even in the first weeks. Before they are capable of pulling the trigger on the gun, they must be instructed in how to use it effectively and safely. The gun is taken apart piece by piece and studied until every function becomes second nature. People who are learning the basics of what they enlisted for are being groomed so that when they have completed the phase of training they are well equipped for duty. God is preparing everyone who believes to do something mighty for Him in His army. It does not matter if you are "in training" or if you are a veteran, anyone can join together in the assembly of believers and lift their voice in prayer. We will not be successful as prayer warriors without other players pulling in the same direction on the same team, because no one can stand alone; it takes the efforts of many to win the victory. The motto of those called to serve on the front line should be, "Two people can accomplish more than twice as much as one; they get a better return for their labor." (Ecclesiastes 4:9) I use that scripture a lot as a reminder and model when I am praying with a group that it is not the work of our hands, but the work of God in our hearts that will accomplish His perfect will.

Questions from the Heart

- Write out what you think a prayer warrior is. Do you agree that there is a difference between a prayer partner and a prayer warrior as it was explained in this chapter?

- Where do you see yourself in your prayer life right now? Do you feel that God is equipping you to stand together for others in prayer?

- Do you have stories of prayer warriors that you know? I encourage you to write these down as a reminder of the important gift they have shared. Have you learned anything by observing their service to God in this way?

- What are some of the points from this chapter that have been relevant to you about explaining what a prayer warrior is?

- Read again the words from Psalms 111:4-5 that were referenced. Can you document where you witnessed God's wonder, grace, or mercy because you have prayed?

Scripture to Rejoice in

Matthew 4:3 & 28:18-19, Colossians 4:2, 1 Peter 10-12, Philippians 2:15-16, Job 11:18
Esther 4:13-17, Psalms 17:1, 1 Samuel 3:10 & 19, 1 Kings 36-37, Daniel 3:16-18, John 3:21

Heart Reflections

Heart Reflections

Chapter Ten

Are You Ready to Raise the Roof?

A Piece of God's Word – "Let us continually offer our sacrifice of praise to God by proclaiming the glory of His name." – Hebrews 13:15

Together we have looked at many aspects of prayer and examined the ways in which we worship and praise God. If you can come into agreement with the reasons God has given us to praise His name, then you are ready to raise the roof and open the flood gates of your heart to experience the wonderful kindness of the Lord. What God has given us is ransom from death, forgiveness of all our sins, and life everlasting through the love of Jesus. That passage from Hebrews 13:15 tells us that every time we speak to others about Christ's name, we are offering Him a sacrifice of praise. Praise is the act of proclaiming God's name as most excellent and high above all else because of His eternal and unchangeable qualities. The people of God are exhorted to use the sounds of singing, music, and voices to cry out with great joy in praise for the gracious provision for our salvation. One-on-one communication with the

Holy Spirit of God must be reached in our worship for it to be effective. In the book of Amos 5:21-24, God says, "I hate all your show of pretense.... Away with your hymns of praise...!" This is a warning that our praise must be sincere and not hypocritical. In worship, the two things that please God are proclaiming the majesty of His name and a pure heart.

Worship, as we concluded through the stories and our study of the scriptures brings us into the presence of God, but it is the growth of our prayer life that keeps us there. This is what the Bible has taught me about prayer. Prayer is an act of humble worship in which we seek God with all our hearts. Prayer is asking God to guide us and then waiting for His direction. Prayer is being willing to discern where it is that God is leading us and accepting His answer. Prayer is assuming that it is possible for us to have an intimate relationship with a God who hears, cares, is righteous, and is able to act. Within that intimate relationship, God will make known His immense love and pours out the resources that are available to us. In summary, God hears our prayers when they are in line with his will. (1 John 5:14) From the examples of the prayer Jesus taught His disciples and the prayer of Jabez we have examined, we see that this is true. James 5:16 assures us that, "A sincere prayer brings wonderful results."

If we want to have an effective prayer life, we need to make sure that we are obedient to some of prayer's fundamental principles. Many of the points introduced individually can now be brought together and placed as lessons into our lives. I have found that I am most confident about the response I receive to prayer when I have submitted first to God's will. I hope these scriptures will also be helpful in encouraging you to see prayer as a vital link to heaven and the best source we have for keeping our spirits lifted. 1 John 1:9 – Prayer often begins with a confession of sin. Philippians 4:6-7 – God invites us to bring our needs and pray to Him about everything. Luke 18:1-8 – Prayer is to be consistent and persistent. Psalm 9:12 – God does not ignore our prayers. Nehemiah 2:4 – Prayer can be beautifully spontaneous. Lastly, 2 Corinthians 12:7-10 – Sometimes we will find that God answers us by giving not what we asked for but by supplying something far better. I promise you, because it is God's Word, that if you seek it, you will find God's wonderful love and wisdom waiting there, ready to be taken.

By searching the Bible and tuning into life experiences, we now have enough information to get us excited and pumped up about turning it up a notch to "raise the roof" with revival passion in our worship, praise, and prayer. Of course we are not going to understand it all now or be able to change everything all at once, but be driven to pick one specific area and go for it! Give it to God and see how far He will take you. Ask as your first prayer of commitment or recommitment that He will show you what can be done on the outside to begin making a change on inside.

At the top of the list of what praise and prayer should accomplish is to transform the union we have with God into a celebration of our life in Jesus Christ. On the night He was betrayed, He shared with us the greatest celebration that we could partake in. The act of the Passover feast that we know as communion was the beginning of understanding the mystery of the good news message: "Jesus came to live in us! God's plan is to make known his secret to his people, this rich and glorious secret which he has for all peoples.

And the secret is that Christ is in you, which means that you will share in the glory of God." (Colossians 1:27) The celebration of this last meal and the elements included demonstrated and revealed how worship was done to fully glorify God for the great things we undeservingly received. As a child of God, this is the whole reason that we can live rejoicing in our Savior! Remind yourself that the Temple of God is our bodies, in which Christ dwells. There is no other god worthy of our attention, adoration, and time. Praising the name of the Lord is how we acknowledge the measure of His love for us. How awesome is it that each one of us has the potential to fulfill the secret of the gospel? It takes my breath away when I meditate and think on that fact. Are you ready to receive such blessings and responsibilities as that?

Understanding Jesus' Prayer at the Last Supper

Revisit with me that last night Jesus spent with His disciplines before His crucifixion. Jesus was almost finished with what He was sent to the world to do. As the hours ticked away on His life, Jesus broke bread with those He called to follow Him. Jesus spent most of the night praying and singing hymns to His heavenly Father. At this point, Jesus was still fully human and aware of what was destined to happen. Never once did He entertain the thought of not fully completing the mission He was sent here to do, which was to save the world. If we are truthful, no matter how good our human intentions are, there is not one of us who might not have been tempted to sneak out of town in the dark of the night to escape the punishment which all sin calls for; death. But because Jesus and the Father are

One, He never questioned what He was given to do. He did it willingly for each one of us because of His great love for us. Let the reality of what Jesus did linger with you. Think about this, God could not have allowed anyone of us to be able to do what Jesus did so purely. If Jesus was not that sacrifice for us, there would be no way of receiving forgiveness for our sins and there would be no salvation. People could never be capable of being their own savior because we are not sinless, only Jesus is without any sin. God in His wisdom gave His only Son the task He alone was capable and worthy of doing.

Jesus' agony in the garden was brought on by the thought of being separated from the Father, not the fear of pain or suffering. His unity with the Father was to be broken because He became sin for us. The consequence of sin is being separated from God and that is what distressed Jesus. We all must hear this point; when Jesus died on the cross, He who knew no sin was to take on the sins of you and me which also separate us from the Father. How did Jesus get through this? The single reason is because He loves us so much that He wants no one to be eternally separated from His Father. Jesus taught us two things from His prayer in the garden. One was that if our prayers stop, that is how we become separated from God and the power of His presence disappears. That knowledge alone should grieve us as much as it did Jesus. Second lesson is Jesus will always remain faithful, so we can place our trust in Him knowing how much we are loved and that He wants to spend time with us in prayer. Since He is the only way to the Father it is important that we stay close to Jesus. It is because He is One with the Father that He was obedient to the Father. The message that Jesus gave the world through the willing sacrifice of giving up His life was that each and every one of us is loved above all things by the Father and the Son. The apostle Mark retells the story of this evening from his view, which was right outside the door to where this moment was unfolding. The entire account being referenced is found in Mark 14:12-26 and Jesus' time in prayer on the Mount of Olives is recorded in Luke 22:39-46. The Holy Bible conceals the whole truth to all who want to know it. We have been given the privilege to go open it.

In the upper room of a small home, Jesus sat down at the wooden table with the twelve men, including the one He knew would betray Him, to prepare the Passover meal. This meal was a custom to remind the Jewish people of the night God spared them because they were faithful and placed the blood of the lamb on their door frames. (Exodus 12:6-11) The meal would become symbolic of Jesus being the unblemished lamb slain for us.

The story comes alive during the meal; Jesus took a loaf of bread and prayed that the Father would bless it. Once the blessing was asked, He broke the bread into pieces. The disciples each took from the loaf as Jesus explained that it was His body that was about to be given up for all. A cup of wine was lifted up as Jesus again prayed, giving thanks first to His Father before He gave it to them to drink. Soon, the wine would turn into His blood, pouring out for many, sealing the covenant between God and His people. Jesus would not drink this cup of wine again until He drank it in His Father's Kingdom. When all this was done, the Son of God sang glad songs of praise. After the meal, Jesus got up and entered the garden to pray. This would also be the place where He was arrested and handed over to the soldiers. Did you notice that Jesus followed His own pattern of prayer during the darkest moment of His life? He asked for God's blessing on the food, He gave all of Himself willingly as an offering to complete God's plan for salvation, and He obeyed God's answer. Most important, Jesus did not go in sorrow; He went forward with praise to bring glory to a mighty God. The gospel of Luke, chapter 22:19, says that when we take the body and blood of Jesus we are to do it with remembrance for what He did.

This account illustrates all I need to know about being joyful, assured, and alive in the Holy Spirit when I pray in the name of Jesus or worship the God of creation! Jesus paid everything for you and me. What now is your answer? Are you ready to *Raise the Roof with Praise and Prayer?*

Questions from the Heart

- What new aspects were revealed to you throughout this study and your personal reflection time concerning what a true heart of praise is or the way in which we need to pray?

- Do you consider yourself to be living out the secret of the gospel? Read Colossians 1:27 again. This is a deeply personal question. Pray about it. Remember, this is only between you and God.

- Using Mark 14:12-26 as your guide, what is significant to you about the offering of the body and blood of Jesus? Have you accepted that He did this for you?

- Jesus told us that when we partake in the meal of communion, we are to do this in remembrance of Him. (Luke 22:19) What are some of the things you remember Jesus for? Do we just receive the gift, or do we take the proper time to thank Him for what it cost Him?

- Have some areas of your spiritual walk been strengthened with renewed freshness to celebrate and use who we are in Christ? Are you ready to raise the bar of how you are raising the roof in your life? How?

Scripture to Rejoice in

James 2:17, Jude 17-20, Ephesians 2:10 & 4:11-13, Isaiah 41:10, James 3:13

Ecclesiastes 4:9-12, Proverbs 27:17, Psalms 37:5, Genesis 39:3, Titus 3:5

Heart Reflections

Heart Reflections

Afterwards

Each time I am privileged enough to search the scriptures and share more of God's message, I am led into deeper insight revealing who it is we serve and more reasons as to why we would want to do it. This time has been no different. As I have reviewed what I have gathered and studied, I have begun to think about praise as being the pulse and prayer as the heartbeat of a fruitful Christian walk. Those are concepts that take some of us years to develop. I challenge you not to overlook them and to strengthen your relationship each day with God. Sing to Him, thank Him, ask Him to bless you, and be wise enough to understand His will for your life. I have been asked, "Well, how am I supposed to know God's will for my life?" What I have learned is that the will God has for all of us is to have faith in Him, and He will be faithful to us. We are promised that God is faithful to those who love Him. (Deuteronomy 7:9) So, if we walk in the love of God, we will be given what we seek. Once our faith believes that God has the best way, we head in the right direction.

If we allow our fears to go unrecognized, sooner or later, they leave us unsettled with doubts and insecurities regarding our self-worth. With the pressures we are asked to face sometimes, fear seems like a natural response. However, I hear my mother-in-law again, as she used to say, "If it isn't worth praying about, then it's not worth worrying about." Since there is nothing we ought to be worried about, this saying was her way of telling us just to pray about it all. She placed everything in prayer and confidently waited for God to supply it. God's word consists of literally hundreds of promises to comfort us in our fears. If we turn on the light of Jesus when we are afraid, we have assurance that He is with us and our fears will fade away. Now that we have collected more tools to use along this journey in life, place the refuge you have found in exploring praise and prayer in your toolbox of things to hold on to. Be ready to pull them out, especially during times of trouble. I believe you will be surprised; the more often we resort to using the gifts God gives us, the more we find that we want to use more of them.

In the closing of this devotional study guide on praise and prayer, it is my sincere prayer that you always stay in the presence of God by praising His name and praying that He draws nearer to you. God shows up mightily in the midst of the worship of His people. "The trumpeters and singers performed together in unison to praise and give thanks to the Lord. Accompanied by trumpets, cymbals, and other instruments, they raised their voices and praised the Lord. At that moment a cloud filled the Temple of the Lord. The priests could not continue their work because the glorious presence of the Lord filled the Temple of God." (2 Chronicles 5:13-14) The key to living now and into eternity is to experience daily the power of the living God. We do not have to let the circumstances that make us feel weak discourage our prayers or tempt us to stop.

Friends, since you have come this far in the journey, you can believe it. Praise the Lord that we can never escape from His Spirit or get away from His presence! (Psalm 139: 1-12)

Once we have secured ourselves with a foundation of salvation and have been brought into friendship with God, we will want to keep it flourishing, healthy, and even protected from damage. In these three books thus far we have introduced a variety of things that you can do to support that relationship. Those methods become our toolbox of tangible items and activities that are there to aide us. We reach for tools all the time to help us complete the jobs we are doing. Our spiritual life needs a toolbox too, so when we are struggling or even when we are not, the tools are there to illuminate our vision and make the work easier. Be thinking about what tools you already have in your box, because we are going to continue filling them up together! Look for the fourth book in the "Mother in Love" series, *Work in Progress… A Toolbox for the Job* to be released in spring 2010.

Until then, be blessed.

About the Author

Mary's stories are taken from the lessons she has been taught in life about the goodness of God and forging a practical relationship with the Holy Spirit. Her past struggles with an eating disorder inspired her to reach out in sharing a message of hope to others that recovery is possible through faith. Mary speaks openly about her struggles and the way God has blessed her life. That time period of struggle, which lasted several years, brought about personal growth, physical healing, and a new spiritual awareness. The experiences that both she and her family went through resulted in the blessing of starting her writing career. Mary published her first magazine article in April 2006 and published her first book in January 2008, titled, *How a Mess Became a Message.*

Her passion is speaking about what God can do in a life. Mary uses the Bible as a daily tool with which she applies its teachings to her life. She has studied the Bible in seminary level classes since 2001 and has been part of small group studies since 1993, providing her with the knowledgeable background she draws upon in writing her daily devotions, studies, and reflections.

Mary has been married since age 19 to the same wonderful man. Together they have been blessed with a son and two daughters. The Barrett family lives in North Wales, Pennsylvania, where they enjoy living in close proximity to many relatives and friends. Some of the hobbies they enjoy are camping in their RV, swimming, going to the beach, visiting loved ones, and enjoying all of God's creations!

Currently, Mary is involved in the "Mother in Love" conference series, which is based on her devotional books. She and her husband Tom are planting the seeds for a ministry they pray God will grow, named Titus II:1 Ministries. This ministry's vision is to bring together all who seek a relationship with the Lord using a variety of outreach methods. There will be more updates about this endeavor as God's plan unfolds. Please feel invited to stay connected with the publications and speaking engagements at www.motherinlove.net.

Lord Hear My Prayer

Lord Hear My Prayer

Lord Hear My Prayer

Lord Hear My Prayer